Hello Code

Book for Programmer
Not Computer

Book Cover by Avrilia

Illustrations by Rosemary

Independently Publishing 2020

Preface: Who is This Book For?

This book is for anyone who is interested in Coding.

If you're looking for a career that's flexible, high-paying, and involves a lot of creative problem solving, software development may be for you.

Of course, each of us approaches our own coding journey with certain resources: time, money, and opportunity.

You may be older, and may have kids or elderly relatives you're taking care of. So you may have less time.

You may be younger, and may have had less time to build up any savings, or acquire skills that boost your income. So you may have less money.

And you may live far away from the major tech cities like San Francisco, Berlin, Tokyo, or Bengaluru.

You may live with disabilities, physical or mental. Agism, racism, and sexism are real. Immigration status can complicate the job search. So can a criminal record.

So you may have less opportunity.

Learning to code and getting a developer job is going to be harder for some people that it will be for others. Everyone approaches this challenge from their own starting point, with whatever resources they happen to have on hand.

But wherever you may be starting out from – in terms of time, money, and opportunity – I'll do my best to give you actionable advice.

In other words: you are in the right place.

A Quick Note on Terminology

Whenever I use new terms, I'll do my best to define them.

But there are a few terms I'll be saying all the time.

I'll use the words "programming" and "coding" interchangeably.

I'll use the word "app" as it was intended – as shorthand for any sort of application, regardless of whether it runs on a phone, laptop, game console, or refrigerator.

I will also use the words "software engineer" and "software developer" interchangeably.

You may encounter people in tech who take issue with this. As though software engineering is some fancy-pants field with a multi-century legacy, like mechanical engineering or civil engineering. And maybe that will be true for your grandkids. But we are still very much in the early days of software development as a field.

I'll just drop this quote here for you:

"If builders built buildings the way programmers wrote programs, then the first woodpecker that came along would destroy civilization." – **Gerald Weinberg**, Programmer, Author, and University Professor

Can Anyone Learn to Code?

Yes. I believe that any sufficiently motivated person can learn to code. At the end of the day, learning to code is a motivational challenge – not a question of aptitude.

On the savannas of Africa – where early humans lived for thousands of years before spreading to Europe, Asia, and the Americas – were there computers?

Programming skills were never something that was selected for over the millennia. Computers as we know them (desktops, laptops, smartphones) emerged in the 80s, 90s, and 00s.

Yes – I do believe that aptitude and interest play a part. But at the end of the day, anyone who wants to become a professional developer will need to put in time at the keyboard.

A vast majority of people who try to learn to code will get frustrated and give up.

I sure did. I got frustrated and gave up. Several times.

But like other people who eventually succeeded, I kept coming back after a few days, and tried again.

I say all this because I want to acknowledge: learning to code and getting a developer job is hard. And it's even harder for some people than others, due to circumstance.

So that is my giant caveat to you: I am not some motivational figure to pump you up to overcome adversity.

There are a ton of people in the developer community who have overcome real adversity. And I'll reference those people later in the book if you want to seek out their teachings.

I'm not seeking to elevate the field of software development. I'm not going to paint pictures of science fiction utopias that can come about if you learn to code.

Instead, I'm just going to give you practical tips for how you can acquire these skills. And how you can go get a good job, so you can provide for your family.

There's nothing wrong with learning to code because you want a good, stable job.

There's nothing wrong with learning to code so you can start a business.

You may encounter people who say that you must be so passionate about coding that you dream about it. That you clock out of your full-time job, then spend all weekend contributing to open source projects.

I do know people who are THAT passionate about coding. But I also know plenty of people who, after finishing a hard week's work, just want to go spend time in nature, or play board games with friends.

People generally enjoy doing things they're good at doing. And you can develop a reasonable level of passion for coding just by getting better at coding.

So in short: who is this book for? Anyone who wants to get better at coding, and get a job as a developer. That's it.

You don't need to be a self-proclaimed "geek", an introvert, or an ideologically-driven activist. Or any of those stereotypes.

It's fine if you are. But you don't need to be.

So if that's you – if you're serious about learning to code well enough to get paid to code – this book is for you.

And you should start by reading this quick summary of the book. And then reading the rest of it.

Hello, Im <CODE/>

Surprising, but true

Early risers are classified into two types:

1. Those using their cellphones before going to the restroom

2. Those using mobile phones in the restroom

Some people read the news, scroll through social media, or work. You have access to the entire world. We've all heard of apps or websites that provide convenience, entertainment, or productivity in our daily lives, but how many of us are aware of the power behind the apps or websites?

Let me introduce "coding." I'm sure the term "coding" is unfamiliar to many people. Despite its current contributions to various sectors ranging from medicine to finance to agriculture, only a few people are interested in learning to code.

It means that the majority of people are customers. As a result, we must introduce coding before it is too late and we realize that we are too preoccupied with sitting back and watching the fast-paced developments.

What is coding?

Coding is how we communicate with computers to assign tasks. Computers, like humans, have a language with which they communicate (computers include all machines: laptops, smartphones and all types of gadgets). We must code in order to communicate with and command computers.

Why do we need to communicate with computer?

Under any circumstances, computers' tireless and emotionally unruffled nature can outperform humans in terms of "getting the job done" efficiently.

Humans, in fact, have far more advantages than computers. However, since computers can assist us, why not give them a shot?

How do online stores support millions of sellers?

How do online taxis outperform a long-established industry?

And there are many other questions, about the strange but real phenomenon that happened because of coding.

How did online marketplaces handle the influx of millions of sellers?

How did online taxis beat a long-established taxi industry?

And there are numerous other questions regarding the occurrence of strange but real phenomena as a result of coding.

Technology took people to the moon many years ago. Technology has also become a part of everyday life and is constantly looking for new problems. Here, now, and then.

If technology is a player on the stage who received a standing ovation, we can now lift the curtain and see coding at work behind the scenes.

Coding has changed people's lives, created jobs, and advanced a country's economy, believe it or not. As a result, there is no reason not to learn more about coding. Isn't coding strange? ... because you weren't aware of it.

The Power of Coding

Each of us has the same 24 hours in a day. You can't buy time no matter how much money you have. Regardless of time constraints, look at the incredible human development in all aspects of life. The contribution of technology to development cannot be separated. We can produce more and better things (money, jobs, or works) with the help of coding than we could without it.

For example now, over 300,000 people are learning coding on *freeCodeCamp* (coding school by *Quincy Larson*), with him also being his teacher.

"How come?"

He teaches on platforms like YouTube, where the video can be watched multiple times without regard for time or location. YouTube is merely a coding product.

In other countries, you can watch *coding* videos at night or in the morning. Consider how long it would take them to teach 300,000 people one at a time if They had to teach them one at a time.

Coding can assist us in breaking free from the 24-hour time constraint concept. Aside from saving time, you will also save energy. When the founder of Facebook purchased Instagram, it had less than 15 employees and millions of users. The number of online marketplace employees is far less than the number of marketplaces.

The same is true for online taxis; the number of drivers far outnumbers the number of users.

The power of coding enables us to automate tasks that must be repeated multiple times, leaving only the work that requires creative thinking and ideas. The most intriguing aspect of coding is that it frequently becomes a medium for one's creativity.

It is a huge mistake to believe that artists aren't cut out for coding; on the contrary, it is a fantastic medium of expression.

Consider that you can create "anything" with lines of writing (coding is required) from your knowledge of the areas you enjoy working with. You can turn ideas in your head into products that you or others can use.

What are the qualifications for becoming a programmer?

A programmer is a person who creates programs or writes code. Many people wonder, "Who is qualified to be a programmer?"

I spent time researching programmers' interests and habits. My discovery was unsurprising: programmers are just like regular people (because they are), and they have diverse hobbies that are vastly different from the perspectives of most people.

Hobbies and habits do not fit into any specific category. There are male, female, child, and adult programmers on every continent, including Asia, Europe, and Africa.

So, what are the qualifications for becoming a programmer? Perhaps the answer is that there are no qualifications.

There is a common misconception that a programmer must be a nerd, someone who is only interested in computers, has no hobbies, and dislikes going outside, as depicted in movies.

Many people are unaware that technologies that make life easier are a hybrid of two distinct fields. Combining automotive and technology, for example, results in a self-driving smart car.

Don't be afraid if you have multiple hobbies; it doesn't mean you don't deserve to be a programmer; it's simply an opportunity for you to combine the two.

Coding is a "tool" that can help you solve problems. You might meet people from medical, literary, financial, urban planning and other areas to use the power of coding to solve problems with the help of technology.

Having no prior experience in information technology

Each of us is a novice at something new. Don't back down simply because you lack knowledge in the field. We are all born from nothing and are therefore weaker than other living beings.

We all have different life stories and ages; some were born first, while others were born later. However, you frequently label yourself as "unworthy" of becoming the person you choose to be.

What if the thought "I'm not good at coding" occurs to you?

I can only picture what if Lionel Messi had the same thought "I'm not good at soccer" or Bill Gates thought "I'm not good at opening vaccine manufacturing facility".

Without them, the world would be less beautiful. Don't let the world have a lack of something just because you think "I'm not good at something".

After all, not all soccer players are as talented as Cristiano Ronaldo, and not all technologists are as brilliant as Steve Wozniak; there is no need to be the best; if you enjoy or can apply a science, begin studying!

You have no control over whether or not you are talented. Don't concentrate on something over which you have no control. Save your energy for exploring and experimenting with new things, such as coding. Did you major in information technology? Or did you hear about it and become intrigued? Whatever brought you here, you have the same chance as everyone else to master coding.

Being labeled as a nerd

In the past, the terms "geek" or "nerd" were used derogatorily to describe people who spent a lot of time on computers. I was initially worried about getting this label, but I realized that people didn't know who I was and that I hadn't introduced myself properly.

I was not ashamed to tell them what I do during daily activities such as sports, family gatherings, or hanging out in cafes; many people are interested in throwing questions and turning into admiration. Many people are eager to learn.

This "geeky" perspective has been slowly changing along with the list of the richest people from the IT industries, such as Bill Gates, Jeff Bezos, Elon Musk, and many more. After knowing these people, do you still think coding is lame?

You need to know that other people are not responsible for the choices you make, nor do they care about your path, other people already have their own problems.

It took blood, sweat, and tears to get it to where it is now. I'm not interested in the stigma; I knew that coding could improve the lives of many people; it doesn't matter if people don't understand coding; my job is to work. Maybe one day my work will be recognized.

The allure of coding

Another reason that coding makes people strange is that people in this world often appear enthusiastic when they meet.

We may be having a deep conversation without being aware of the presence of other people around us.

On the plus side, not everyone in other fields can be passionate about their work, indicating a deep love for their profession.

Most people are unaware that when we code, we unconsciously enter a state of flow. A flow state is a mental state in which a person is completely focused and productive.

This sensation is sometimes referred to as being "in the zone" by some. Consider Diego Maradona dribbling over his opponent or Tiger Woods hitting a hole-in-one. A programmer is frequently in this exceptional state. Understandably, some people spend a significant amount of time on computers to express their creativity without being compensated.

They typically display tech logo stickers on their laptops as a source of pride, engage in programming discussions on social media platforms, are involved in urban communities, and so on. These are indications that many people enjoy coding rather than just doing it for a living.

You may not like it at first, but once you "get it," it's difficult not to.

Reasons to Explore the World of Coding

Before attending college, I was one of those people who didn't know what I wanted to be, didn't understand, and was often afraid of who I would become.

Because I knew some seniors, I decided to major in mechanical engineering in college. So, this was a safe bet because I am hoping that they would assist me when I had problems. In fact, it was not what I expected; a letter arrived informing me that I had been rejected for mechanical engineering, and I couldn't hide my sadness. additionally, the feeling of fear returned, reminding me of an increasingly uncertain future.

I went to Germany to study in 2006. I couldn't just walk into a faculty. Instead, I had to spend a year in a preparatory class called StudienKolleg.

Later, the StudienKolleg score would determine what major and course to enroll in; no more entrance exams.

I tried coding for the first time in the second semester of the preparatory class, learning to create programs using the command prompt terminal application, an unattractive, text-only application.

I wrote simple programs that converted hours to seconds and Celsius to Fahrenheit. To tell the truth, it was love at first sight.

Despite my interest, I chose mechanical engineering because it made me feel safer.

My second choice was to major in informatics.

Fortunately, the rejection letter arrived, and the sadness quickly turned to gratitude. After studying for a few semesters, I gradually became interested in the world of coding after witnessing its power.

Just because I enjoy it does not guarantee that everything will go smoothly.

When I applied for an internship at a company in my fifth semester, I received an email informing me that I had dropped out of college after failing a subject three times.

Worrying about the future, as well as disappointing my parents and being embarrassed to meet friends, brought back the same fear.

But who decides "what will I become?" the university or myself? The latter is unquestionably the correct answer.

I was enthusiastic about this field and decided to pursue it further. I no longer get frustrated with studying effectively and instead learn about what interests me. I choose my own study time and topic. I studied the materials, continuing to pursue my interests.

I created my own curriculum from various sources, read books in the library, and searched the internet for endless information.

I'd never studied with such zeal before. My confidence gradually returned, and I found the courage to apply for jobs as a programmer, not once or twice, but more than a dozen times to various companies in Canada and Berlin, Germany.

I frequently slipped a message stating that I was willing to work for free because the most important thing was to gain experience. My desire to learn was extremely strong.

freeCodeCamp

In my spare time, some college friends studying coding asked me to teach them. What am I? I was pessimistic. I didn't even finish college, let alone teach coding. My friends' enthusiasm, on the other hand, inspired me to teach them. I also shared my knowledge with them because many of them struggled to understand coding.

My wishes came true gradually, one by one. I got a job in Berlin despite having no degree, and, more interestingly, they were willing to pay! I began to feel more secure, and I felt more confident in doing other things.

I went to college while studying online at freeCodeCamp. From here, I began to meet many people in the same field, learn from them, and share experiences.

A few years later, freeCodeCamp unexpectedly became my intermediary in earning income.

To this point, I am still interested in learning new programming skills and putting them into practice in order to create a product that many people can use.

I also teach others about what I've learned. This is what keeps me in the coding world. I'm not sure why you've decided to enter the world of coding. Your parents may have forced you to attend college, or you may have simply followed your peers.

It's possible that you have different motivations for diving in and staying motivated. All I can say is that the power of coding has the potential to change the fates of many people, beginning with your own.

The other side of programming

I see coding as a combination of many components, including the art component, which requires you to write beautiful code that is easy to maintain and read, the engineering component, which requires you to ensure the program works, and the creativity component. There are many ways to do things, and you can find one that is very different from others.

It also has a psychology component, in which you consider how to make users want and feel comfortable using your program, as well as a kindness component, in which you use your program to make people's lives easier. There are numerous other components that help with coding and vice versa. You need to reconsider if you believe that programming is a rigid job performed by stiff people!

Connecting the dots

I recall the first time I encountered programming. After being taught some basic theories, we were asked to write a function with the output that says *"hello"*, often referred to as *'Hello World'*. I was astounded that I could command the computer to do whatever I wanted.

Most people rarely experience such feelings because they understand the theory but do not put it into practice.

This is my basis for learning in FreeCodeCamp hands-on, I also suggest them to study there, so that others can experience the same magic that I did years ago.

If programming material is only presented through presentations, it can become tedious. Because they haven't seen the creative side of the coding world, many people give up and decide to despise it. Every lesson has a theory, and programming is no different.

Variables, functions, classes, Object Oriented Programming, and other topics must be introduced to beginners. As a learner, you may look at the materials as dots, like stars in the sky, and connect the dots with lines to form beautiful constellations.

We can't build anything without the theoretical dots. It's normal to need to ask questions or read more if something doesn't make sense. In a forum or in class, don't be afraid to ask what the material is being taught for.

It will be easier to take the lessons if you know what you want to achieve. To be sure, patience is required, you will only be able to build a picture once you have a large number of dots. The dots represent the theories that are required.

A note to teachers: in order to balance theory and practice, creativity is required. Remember to inform students that the theories will be useful for specific purposes.

Is English important?

Is English really necessary here?

Yes, English is necessary.

Is it true that if you don't speak English, you can't code?

Not really, but knowing English, even if only passively, can provide many advantages (being able to read or understand English content). The majority of literacy books, Q&A forums, and learning content, including programming language documentation, are written in English. Many people are gradually volunteering to create or translate content into their native languages. However, when you rely on others, content translation is difficult and time-consuming. As a result, it is strongly advised that you begin learning English seriously and set aside money and time to do so. Learning English not only opens the door to coding, but also to other areas of knowledge. You will not be sorry.

We live in a world where people can easily exchange ideas through the internet. English is the world's unifying language. To understand what people are talking about and even contribute to the conversation, you must speak English.

Consider this: if you encounter a problem and want to find a solution on the internet, the chances are that the problem has already been asked or discussed by someone in this world.

Therefore, typing keywords in English into a search engine like Google may increase your chances of solving the problem. The same is true for learning something new; whether through videos, articles, or podcasts, there are numerous resources available in English.

Having a study partner is the most effective method, you may join a course or community in your area. Don't be shy, regardless of your age, you are the only person who will benefit from this investment. You can also download English learning apps that you can use whenever you want. All roads led to Rome!

I was terrible at math

When I was in college, there was one subject that I avoided at all costs: chemistry. I tried to get out of every chemistry class as quickly as possible. The most important thing was that I passed the class.

In contrast to math, my relationship with math is quite unique. I've always been confident in my math skills, but I often get bad grades on tests.

"I'm not good at math," is another common complaint among people who want to learn to code. My response is "me too!"

Math is one of the basic sciences, along with reading and writing, because almost all of the jobs we will do will require math.

The good news is that you don't have to be a math "expert" to be good at coding. However, if you are an expert, it is a plus.

In some cases, we may need to use more complex math formulas to complete tasks. I recall getting a college assignment that required me to convert an image to black and white or detect faces, similar to the technology used by some social media platforms. We were given the formula to use in order to create these features.

The task was to convert the formula into variables in coding. You are not developing the formula from scratch, but rather converting the original formula into lines of code.

Unlike English, which has a higher priority and a longer learning process, it won't take long to learn basic math. Therefore, it is worthwhile to begin learning math again, just give it a few weeks or a month to learn the basics of math.

Depending on the focus you choose, your career may require advanced math skills.

For example, if you want to learn Machine Learning or Data Science, you might need to understand more complicated math than just the fundamentals.

The solution is the same, you "just" need to learn. Drop everything if you think you're bad at math. Be a beginner once more. Learn from scratch. Why can't you start from scratch if everyone else does?

Other subjects

In general, there are numerous fields in the world of work. When working at a large online store, You must be familiar with e-commerce merchant issues. If you're working in a lab and need to visualize and read data from a study, you'll need to know what the study is about.

This job will always intersect with other jobs, so don't be surprised if you come across something new.

You don't have to be an expert in the field, but you must be willing to learn about the problem you're attempting to solve.

My senior reminded me of his favorite quote *"those who want, will find a way. Those who don't, will find an excuse"*.

We can either complain about not understanding a particular subject or use the various conveniences we have, such as the internet, to begin learning about it.

Remember that the goal is not to become an expert, but to comprehend the subject to provide solutions in the form of a program.

I don't memorize anything about the programming language

Another reason people give up is that they believe they will be unable to memorize the program language's commands. The good news is that you don't have to memorize them.

In fact, almost all lessons do not require memorization. However, the learning method in school is a bit different, and schools often require you to memorize mass amounts of information. The grading system at school is the issue. People are forced to memorize information that does not need to be remembered.

In the real world, you can seek assistance from Google.

We've all heard of Stack Overflow, a website that serves as a platform for users to ask and answer questions that people have been looking for for years.

We're not being asked to memorize anything because, if that's all there is to it, Google is far smarter. The ability to think about problem-solving through coding is required.

So, what should we do?

The answer is "to understand".

Understanding is often underestimated as a result of common grading systems, such as multiple choice, which can play guessing games without caring whether or not the student has understood.

How do you know if you've grasped the concept?

You can tell if you have grasped the concept by attempting to explain it back to others or by putting it into practice. Fortunately, in the world of programming, the cost of putting knowledge into practice isn't expensive, all we need is a platform to write code and simulate it.

So, unlike in some other fields, practice is not something that can be accomplished alone.

When learning a new concept, consider whether you understand it or have simply memorized it. If you simply memorize, the evolving program language will render your memory obsolete in the future.

You may be able to pass exams by rote in school, but the working world is very different. Understanding a concept has the advantage of allowing you to learn more than one programming language and other technologies in the future. This will be a simple task.

You'll be a versatile fighter who can switch between weapons.

How to master coding fast?

It's a secret formula. Since you're reading this book, I'll just tell you how to master coding fast.

1. Take about 3/4 cup of water
2. Splatter it all over your face
3. Keep in mind that nothing happens in an instant.

Hey! You can't learn something overnight. Stop looking for an easy way to get something. Don't be fooled by phrases like "master coding in 3 hours", mastering the skill takes much longer.

You must be eager to learn, not just read or watch tutorials, but to actually LEARN. Trying to grasp something.

When was the last time you did something like this?

We are accustomed to chasing grades and passing exams in school. There is no exam this time, you decide whether or not to study and whether or not to have the skills.

Naval Ravikant, an investor once said *"easy choice, hard life"*, followed by *"hard choice, easy life"*.

There are many temptations along the way, and we are drawn to play like other friends or join every family invitation to watch and enjoy other entertainment. These are simple options with immediate gratification, but the cost will be your life. On the other hand, if you make the difficult decisions now, such as devoting time to your studies, your life will be easier.

What should I learn?

The world of coding is vast. Asking what you should learn is like coming to the airport and asking "where should I go?".

There are many program languages, just as there are many human languages. The first step is to decide what you want to do, whether it's building websites, developing Android apps, connecting IoT (Internet of Things) machines, or something else entirely.
Once you've decided what you want to explore, you can start asking people or searching the internet in that context. Example: "Hi... Where should I begin if I want to become an iOS app developer?".
It's a lot more helpful than asking "I want to learn to code … what should I learn?".

Coding has a wide range of applications.
The program language or tool you must use is not mentioned in this book on purpose because it is dynamic and subject to change.

Don't worry, you can get detailed answers from the internet or people.

The grass on the other side of the fence is greener.

Concentrate on your studies once you've decided what you want to study. If you don't, it's easy to be swayed by other people's opinions and advice that isn't right for you.

It is not necessary to learn everything, and it is impossible to learn everything. You must make a decision and strive to be consistent in your learning.

People will shout, "Learning A is better" or "Learning B is more important," but keep in mind that all advice is context-dependent.

Don't just read the blog title, find out why they came to that conclusion. The grass on the other side of the fence is much greener. You'll be enticed to go there. Forget about the grass you've been mowing on your own lawn.

There are numerous methods for learning

Nobody knows your best learning method better than you. There are numerous ways to learn, including written articles, videos, and direct learning opportunities such as on campus, bootcamp, or courses.

I can give advice, and so can others, but remember that the best way to learn is back to you, so don't swallow the advice whole.

Phased or hands-on project creation

You can learn from the curriculum that is available online. Typically, you may be introduced to the material one by one. This is good for laying a solid foundation and broadening your knowledge of a subject.

However, most people are impatient to make something right away, believing that the material delivered one by one is tedious.

The second option is to create a hands-on project. There is such a learning system, where we can learn about the material and the issues encountered while working on the project.

I've seen people learn faster this way, deciding that they want to make "A", then slowly learning the small components of "A".

Online or Offline

You don't have to choose this option because you can do both. There are numerous lessons to be found both online and in the real world. There are numerous options for online learning, ranging from people voluntarily sharing information on their blogs to large universities freely sharing their learning   videos.

I recommend that you "know" what you want first, because otherwise, cyberspace can become a weapon, where you learn something that is not fit for purpose indefinitely.

Determine what you need before learning the technical material.

Keywords to start researching and entering into search engines:

"How to create a website"

"How to create an android app"

"How to create an iOS app"

"How to become a data scientist" and so on...

Collect several references to help you expand your knowledge of the subject you want to master. This will help you avoid learning incorrect information.

There are also numerous opportunities for face-to-face learning, such as study groups, communities, bootcamps, and universities.

Let's go over them one by one.

College

Attending college is a popular option There's nothing wrong with going to college if you have the means, either financially or in terms of living conditions. However, make sure it is what you truly want rather than what your parents want you to do.

*Please keep in mind that what you believe to be good can be bad, and vice versa. If you disagree with your family, instead of becoming angry or sad, Inquire about their intentions and express your desires.

The benefit of attending college is that you will eventually obtain a degree. Some people, particularly parents, feel more secure when they can show degrees and diplomas.
Personally, I don't believe this is the most important factor in selecting a college.

The most significant benefit is that you will meet people who share your interests, they can be your playmates and study buddies, and a few will become your work buddies.

Because you meet them more frequently, it is easier to share ideas and plan activities together.

Take advantage of your opportunity to ask the lecturer critical questions in class. Don't take anything at face value because there are so many learning resources available. Instead, before entering the lecture, pose questions that you believe are interesting and can be discussed in class.

I learned a lot from college friends who are also self-taught in cyberspace, they became far superior to their classmates, the tasks appears to be simple, and eventually, preparing a thesis was no longer a burden. It could lead to the birth of a real project used by real users.

Study group

You can do it whether you're in college or not. College students have an advantage because they already know people who share their interests.

Small study groups are essential for keeping you motivated. After all, you just 'listen' without evaluation in college, and it takes a long time to wait for an exam to test your knowledge.

Don't wait for an "expert" to come along. People who are eager to learn are required to form a study group. The group's goal is to learn, not to teach. So, if you don't believe you're intelligent, there's no need to feel overburdened. It's called a learning group, not a teaching group.

Join a community

On a broader level, when your study group becomes overcrowded, it's time to form a community.

Communities are typically associated with limiting the scope of technology or being from a specific city (but don't limit yourself). The goal of a community is to make scheduled "events", such as a seminar with a keynote speaker or a hacking simulation event.

The community requires organizers, individuals who are willing to sacrifice their time to think about the community. Total members may increase from a combination of several study groups or students from different campuses.

There are both online and offline communities. Joining an offline community will allow you to meet many people in person.

What if there are no communities in your city? Begin building your community!

Join a general cyberspace group like Facebook or Telegram, then ask if anyone is from city 'x,' and from there you can start your own community.

Bootcamp or course

Those with more financial means can apply to a bootcamp or course. The benefit of bootcamp is that you can consult with expert teachers or mentors at any time. Because there are fewer students on bootcamp than on campus, it is easier to have a discussion.

Particular bootcamps provide free education but require payment after you've landed a job. For individuals who want to learn hands-on, this is a win-win situation for both parties.

Each bootcamp may provide different services, some may deduct a percentage of your salary, while others may charge a flat fee. You should inquire about specifics before enrolling to avoid misunderstandings.

HackaLearn

Do you ever feel like you don't have time to study? This is one option. I was first approached by a community friend, Robert Olivier, who is very active in sharing information in my hometown of Denver.

Despite being a newcomer, I am always impressed by his enthusiasm. We were talking about something one day when the question came up "what if we study at the same time of day and have to present it in the afternoon?".

What problems does the above learning concept solve?

First, the passion of individual learning differs from that of group learning. Second,There is a deadline or time limit within which you must present it. Thus, to explain a material, you must first learn it, not simply pretend to read it.

You can learn anything, and each individual can select different materials. If the materials are the same, you can study in groups with a focus on one theme for half a day or more to gain new knowledge.

I took the name Hackalearn from 'hackathon' and 'learning'.

Whereas the common goal of a hackathon is to complete a project in a few days, this time, the goal is to learn.

Reading the code

Maria Popova is a blog writer known for her ability to weave words, quotes, and stories from real people of all ages into a single cohesive article. When Maria was asked who she was, she replied "a reader who writes".

Although she is well-known for her writing, she never forgets that all of her writings are the result of her love of reading.

You may try to start reading, not just articles, but also code written by others, such as code from seniors in the office, on campus, or on the internet. You can learn a lot from them, and you can use this code as inspiration or direct knowledge to create your next program.

Websites like github allow us to see other people's code. Almost all programs written in various languages have their source code available on github.

Websites like github, allow us to see the code that other people have. Almost all programs from various types of languages have their code on github.

Have you ever read another person's code? If not, try it now. It will open your mind, perhaps that person learned a tip you haven't heard before.

When you're looking for an answer to a problem, such as on the Stack Overflow site, the coding school forum, or other programming groups, and someone else shares the answer, you have the opportunity to read the one's code.

You won't learn anything new if you just copy the code, so try to read carefully what they wrote.

Others' code is not always flawless, so you must consider why the person wrote it and whether there is a better way of writing a code. If you have a better or more efficient way of writing a code, don't be afraid to tell the code owner.

You are a writer

On the other hand, you are a writer and coder. Someone, at the very least your future self, will read the code you write someday. For this reason, rather than simply running code on a computer, you should write code that is easy for humans to read.

THE ONLY VALID MEASUREMENT OF CODE QUALITY: WTFS/MINUTE

If you are working on a project and some lines of code need to be changed or you want to create new lines of code in a year, understanding the meaning of the lines of code will be difficult if your code is messy and random. As a result, writing easy-to-read code will benefit you at the very least.

Steal like an artist

A lack of confidence often occurs in starting to write, especially when confronted with an empty text-editor. **Austin Kleon**, author of *'Steal Like an Artist,'* suggests that "stealing" can help your creativity.

What kind of stealing is it?

Austin implies that you can take or copy other people's work while learning because doing so will help you figure out where to start.

Many times, our ideas come to us after we start working on a piece, no matter how unattractive it may be at first. A true artist, on the other hand, does not simply copy, they use the work of others as a learning material.

Those who want to learn will find inspiration. Teachers and codes are now widely available on the internet, you can choose whether or not to learn.

Learn to ask questions

Whether you like it or not, you will face difficulties in your studies. To get out of this situation, you must learn to ask good questions.

If you've ever been to a programming group, you'll notice that there are some places where many newcomers are surprised because when they ask questions, they receive negative responses.

Negative responses are undesirable, but mistakes frequently occur because beginners are overly lazy to read the rules of the game established by the group or community owner.

Here are some tips for asking a good question:

1. Read the rules

Assume you have a playground and set some ground rules for it. If a new person breaks the rules, the owner will be upset.

When you join a group or a forum, read the rules thoroughly because you are entering someone else's garden.

2. **Look for previous questions.**

To find answers to your questions, use search engines such as Google. Because this is not a new topic, chances are that someone has already asked the same question. People may get mad when they have to answer or repeat the same question.

3. **Give it a catchy title.**

Write down the gist of your question so that people can get an idea of what you want to ask before delving into your problem in depth. Make sure the title is easily read by humans, rather than simply writing "please fix the error" or "help with the assignment", others perceive this as a sign of laziness because you do not take the time to understand the issue. You're just yelling for help.

4. Describe the issue

Next, describe your problem in an organized manner:

    a. what are you making?

    b. what is your desired outcome?

    c. what is the current situation?

Problems that arise without a clear context may receive inappropriate solutions.

Don't forget to tell others how to find the error, which is known as reproducing the bug.

5. Include code or screenshots

Include your code to facilitate others in finding the problem, there's no need to upload the entire folder or show all the pages, just the error part.

Instead of just writing it down, screenshots can help you visualize what's the situation.

6. **When you're finished, share your solution**.

When we ask a question, we frequently find the solution before anyone responds. I often see a pattern of people deleting the question or simply writing [solved] or done. This is a selfish act. If you asked, you should be willing to share the answer, tell me even if you made a blunder.

Someone may be in the process of solving your problem or may face the same problem in the future. Don't leave questions unanswered. If you ask, be prepared to answer.

"To be reluctant to make in queries will make one go astray"
We often hear this proverb, but there is another one that we can use in coding: "Ask more, get lost less".

You may ask questions on website forums so that they can be read by search engines rather than chat groups that will get lost over time. This will help a lot of other people who are dealing with similar problems in the future. When you find something interesting in the group chat, you can turn it into a blog post that more people can read.

There's a funny story about a programmer who encountered a problem, then searched on Google, only to discover that the solution he discovered was his own writing from some time ago.

Like to make excuses

People often make excuses and blame others for their mistakes.

"I didn't go into programming because I couldn't do the math."

"I didn't study because I didn't have a laptop"

"I'm not sure where to begin, I'll do it later"

You might have more excuses to keep you calm for a while, excuses not to study, but they're just like watching entertainment, it won't last long.

You'll come to regret not starting to study sooner.

"The best time to start studying was yesterday. The second best time is today"

I have poor logic skills

" I have poor xyz skills"

You can replace "xyz" with any subject, math, English, logic, or other subjects. You'll always make excuses for not studying because you have poor skills. Instead, you should say "I'm bad at math... therefore I will study math". Add the phrase 'therefore I will study…' in your subsequent complaint.

People employ logic as an abstract term when they are unable to solve a problem. We often overlook the missing pieces and draw inferences; if I can't do A, then I can't do Z, just like individuals wishing to go from points A to Z without considering the letters B to Y.. actually we often eliminate what is lacking, we often draw conclusions, because I can't be A then I can't be Z

Algorithms are often associated with programming. Algorithms are the steps we take to complete tasks.

As an example,

Algorithm of how to get to school:

- Prepare supplies and wear school uniforms
- Go to the bus station
- Take the bus to school

Algorithm of how to fry the chicken:

- Marinate the chicken with spices
- Let it stand for a while
- Heat the oil

- Deep fry the chicken for 5 minutes

I could provide plenty of such examples. The bottom line is that in order to complete a task, certain steps must be taken, which we might refer to as the logic or algorithm.

Also, each activity may have a separate algorithm. For example, when going to school, some students may need to cross the bridge, or in the case of fried chicken, some may need to purchase the chicken if it is not already available. A single task can be completed in a variety of ways.

To achieve the desired outcome, programming requires breaking down a problem into steps known as algorithms. Generally speaking, when people say that you have poor logical skills, they fail to break down the problem and solve it one step at a time.

As of now, when you have a problem, try to break it down into small components and progressively solve the previously impossible problem.

I didn't go to IT college

If you didn't go to IT college, the good news is that you don't have to worry, because you are not required to have a student card to access the internet or join the community.

Don't be confused, now there are KhanAcademy, freeCodeCamp and many more for those of you who don't go to college

There are benefits to attending university (discussed in the section on study methods), but this is not an excuse not to study. It would be unfortunate if all those people who did not have the opportunity to attend university, whether due to tuition fees, location, or other reasons, could not pursue a career in this line of work.

If you cannot afford it or prefer not to attend college, you are not alone; there are many people who did not study informatics but nevertheless managed to have a good career. There are individuals who were unable to attend college, those who attended but dropped out, and those who majored in other fields but still obtained employment in the IT industry.

How do you do it? There is no other way than to learn. As long as you want to study, the internet and learning communities are available to assist you. See the 'learning methods' section for more alternative learning resources.

Pretend to be a college student

Not many people know (except IT students) that not all college students understand the materials in college. Some students pay someone to do their assignments or purchase diplomas. I'm sure you've heard about it.

For college students who are solely interested in obtaining a degree, "Why do you want to spend your precious time just to be praised by others?"

When you graduate, you will be alone, and people will return to their own issues and businesses.

If you are offended, calm down, It doesn't mean you're out of luck; how long do you want to deceive others? You can't fool yourself by appearing to have a degree or several certificates but no real talents. You will suffer. Begin learning with the goal of gaining knowledge that you can put to use.

Don't have the time

Everyone in this world has the same amount of time, 24 hours a day, from toddlers to the old. The excuse of not having enough time is our way of expressing, "I have more important things to do.

In a nutshell, we have chosen to prioritize other tasks. However, our priorities are not always in our best interests.

"Time is what we want most, but what we use worst." - William Penn

Deciding to learn means setting aside time for it. *Tim Ferris* says "if it's not on your calendar, it's not real".

Therefore, your first step is to free up time to begin studying. Make a learning schedule based on your needs and activities, whether it's in the morning, midday, or late at night. Making a schedule is useless if you don't follow through.

Is learning to code important to you? If the answer is yes, then make time for it.

Programmers are loners

I'm not sure why the stereotype of programmers as loners is so common. Despite my observations, programmers have a sizable community and frequently congregate. It's a different scenario when you're working; for some people, including myself, quiet settings are essential. Maybe the assumption arises from seeing programmers working alone for complete concentration. This is, in my opinion, a positive development that should be echoed in other sectors.

Whether the statement above is true or not, solitary moments can often be considered unfavorable. However, I personally enjoy having personal moments in the midst of my job, community, and family-related activities. I can use the solitary moments to learn something new or reflect on what I've done today with complete self-awareness.

In the area of programming, the community is a highly comparable phenomenon, and many seniors advise entering and building a community. They understand that it is difficult for individuals to progress if they have no support from an ideal setting for learning. There is no seniority in the community; you can ask questions and offer assistance.

No one helps

You're the one who isn't putting forth enough effort. Communities exist in both the virtual and physical worlds these days. Make the most of your efforts to locate these communities, and don't be afraid to attend an event; any person gets nervous the first time. When you do have the guts to attend, don't squander it by 'simply watching' without asking questions or, more importantly, introducing yourself to others.

Video streaming sites, search engines, and Q&A forums will always be there to assist you. Remember that behind every written article or video tutorial is a real person assisting you. You will never be alone.

If you already have some knowledge, don't be afraid to share it with others, whether through writing, videos, or coaching other juniors. We can get here because of those who came before us.

Not having a laptop

Not everyone has the same opportunities. Some people are born into wealthy households, while others are not. We cannot change our birth conditions, all we can do is try to improve our current situation.

*The history of the beginning of "**Mas Sugeng Template**" edited the code from the cellphone, until he was able to buy a computer*

I often hear about programmers who started out as internet cafe attendants. Other than earning some cash, this is also an opportunity to spend time with computers (not for playing games). This can be a solution for you who lack the gear to get started, you do not have to work at an internet café, but you can rent a computer from one.

It is pointless to whine about your condition if you do not currently have enough money to purchase a laptop or computer. It would be considerably more beneficial if you:

1. Start working. It doesn't have to be a professional job, as long as it's halal and you earn money, you may save it to buy your own gadgets. Go to shops or food stalls, and inquire whether they need assistance with anything from washing dishes to lifting goods.

2. Learn programming at an internet cafe. Renting is likely less expensive than buying at first. You can store your learning progress by purchasing a USB drive or using cloud storage.

Learn how to make money

It's not a bad idea to learn how to work. Remember that you are not required to work professionally from the very beginning. Any job will suffice. It will broaden your perspective and make you appreciate the efforts of others who have assisted you over the years.

Having money allows you to understand how to prioritize where you spend your money, such as seminars, programming classes, English courses, and so on. All of these are costly investments. The term "investment" refers to the possibility that what you spend today will multiply the results in the future.

Laptops are only your first excuse

Don't be mistaken, it's human nature to complain and seek out what does not exist. When you have your own computer, you might need another device that you do not presently possess.

This is a basic human trait that must be recognized and avoided.

Be grateful for what you have, and only purchase or wish for anything when you truly need it or it will make your work more effective. But don't assume that just because you don't have a 'x' device means you can't work.

But I'm a girl

"It's the mark of a backward society - or a society moving backward - when decisions are made for women by men." - Melinda Gates

In the area of technology, diversity is a hot topic. There is a widespread misconception that informatics is only for men. When women study or work in this sector, they are always regarded as odd. In fact, way back in the early history of computers, there was a woman named Ada Lovelace known as the first programmer in the world! **(not the first female programmer).**

She once wrote about a machine, and her concept was that this machine could be more than just a mathematical computation tool. It all happened back when machines were not as sophisticated as they are now, and women were considered to make little contribution.

Thus, it is not worth it for women to feel inferior or to be terrified to enter the area of informatics because history cannot be changed, women have successfully won the past, why not the future?

Ada Lovelace

More importantly, the goal of technology is to make humans' lives easier. Guess what... are humans solely made up of men, or do women exist as well? Obviously, the latter.

When we wish to use technology to simplify the difficulties of all parties, it goes without saying that the solution maker must come from both parties.

Solving a problem from a single point of view has drawbacks. In simple terms, it is not only women who require the assistance of technology, but technology also requires the assistance of women.

I have an online acquaintance named Katia.

She used to be a baker, but now she works as a programmer at Microsoft...

And here's the story about her...

From Baker to Software Engineer at Microsoft in 2 Years (by Katia)

In 2018 I was working overtime hours at a bakery. Every day I would come in, decorate cakes and cookies and provide customers with their sugary cravings. Even though this job was creative and fun, there were many monotonous tasks and over time I decided I wanted to do something that would prove to be more challenging.

Bet you can guess what happened.

I started learning programming in my free time as a hobby. Well, that hobby quickly turned into a much-wanted career. I would be daydreaming at my bakery shifts about the time running by so that I could rush home and learn something new.

Pretty soon I quit my job and started teaching myself programming full time. I quickly realized that if I wanted to ramp up quickly and land a job, I needed a bootcamp program to provide that quick acceleration. A couple weeks before the completion of the program I landed my first developer job in Denver, Colorado. Fast forward a year later...

At the end of 2019, I applied for the LEAP apprenticeship program at Microsoft and got in! Once the apprenticeship program ended, I was offered a full time position to continue working with the current team.

Now, I'm telling you this story hoping that it will inspire you and make you realize that anything you set your mind to is possible.

However, accomplishing these things wasn't easy. It would be a lie to tell you it wasn't hard work. But I am here to give you some tips if you are starting off programming and want to accelerate quickly.

Be Prepared for Hard Work

Not a lot in life comes easy. Programming is not easy to get started with. You must put in the hours of learning to accelerate. There is a huge need for developers and engineers in the tech industry, but getting your first job will be your biggest hurdle. If you decide that software engineering will be the career path you decide to follow, remember it is a life time of learning and hard work.

Concentrate on One Concept/Language At a Time

When I was first getting started, I spent a lot of time reading articles on the Internet about different programming languages . I'm not proud to say that I switched around a lot. After a few months of self learning I knew some basics of Python, JavaScript, and Ruby. Was it enough knowledge in those languages to actually complete a project? Absolutely not. I highly encourage you to choose one language and stick to it. Master one language and others will follow suite a lot easier. With programming there are endless opportunities to learn new concepts. Take one course/book, finish it, and move on to the next.

Be a "YES" Man/Woman

Stop making excuses for yourself. Also, never be afraid to take on something that you don't feel comfortable doing. If there is a project that someone is asking you to complete, but you decline it because you don't feel technically prepared, you are closing down doors to career growth. Let me tell you a little secret. You will never feel fully prepared to take something on. When you take on something you aren't sure you can do, you are learning more than ever. You are challenging yourself instead of staying in a comfort zone. Now, this doesn't mean take on 25 projects at work and drown in work.

Projects, Projects, and more Projects

I'm betting you right now, if you are a beginner you will skip right over this paragraph. If fact, you'll probably say: *"YES, YES, KATIA, I KNOW PROJECTS ARE IMPORTANT FOR BECOMING A SOFTWARE ENGINEER BUT I NEED TO FINISH A COURSE AND GET A BETTER UNDERSTANDING OF WHAT I'M LEARNING. ONCE I'M MORE COMFORTABLE, I'LL START BUILDING PROJECTS"* . You can watch as many tutorials as you want and you might learn quite a bit, but until you have hands on the keyboard your progress will not reach its fullest potential. If you need project ideas and don't know where to start you can comment below and I'll respond with some great easy things you can start out with.

Making Sacrifices With Your Time

There is a lot of ways to spend your free time. You should always find time to relax and have fun no matter how hard you are working. But at the same time, if you have huge future goals, you have to put in the time to see the results. When I was learning to program, I was dating a guy who would be out with his friends every weekend. I always wanted to tag along, but instead I disciplined myself to stay home and spend those hours learning. It was so hard to not partake in the fun at the time. Looking back on it, I am more than glad that I worked hard and made those sacrifices. Those sacrifices helped me land my first job.

Don't Ever Get Too Comfortable

I notice a lot of people get a new job and all of a sudden they get very comfortable. They have no interest in learning anything outside of their job scope requirements. Don't be that person! Always have goals. Carve out time on the job to learn something new. See yourself growing within the company, or moving on to bigger aspirations. I didn't go from baking to software engineering by staying comfortable. I was constantly working and dreaming of bigger and better goals.

You Have to Take Risks

Many parts of my journey in the last two years have been taking huge risks. Quitting my job at the bakery was a risk. Taking on a very challenging assignment at my first job was a risk. The biggest risk was quitting my stable job for an 3 month apprenticeship at Microsoft that did not guarantee employment. This goes hand in hand with being comfortable. I was comfortable working at the bakery, but was I happy with my job and career? Absolutely not. Was I worried about switching to a newer much more challenging career path? Absolutely. Big risks can yield big successes.

I hope that you are now motivated to go learn and pursue your career ambitions. I love sharing my story with others. It shows that if you put your mind to something you will reap the results. We live in a time where the Internet is so accessible. There is nothing stopping you from starting to learn. There are so many free resources, blog posts, videos. The sky is your limit.

****
****

So that's the story of the baker who opted to 'burn bridges' in order to become a programmer and eventually got her dream job...

Age Limit

This is a frequently asked question: what age is appropriate for coding? The answer is 3-6 months old, when they are still newborns.

Just kidding!

There is no specific age at which you should begin. Don't be concerned with trivialities like age until you've determined why you want to code and what you want to create with it. When you want to learn to code or build programs, no one cares how old you are. Obviously, If the question is what age is the minimum for working in a company, the answer will be different because this criterion differs per company.

But, when it comes to learning and building programs, don't say "I'm too young, I'll do it later" or "well, I'm too old, I think coding doesn't suit me" from now on. It's just one of many grumbles to come.

Here's a fascinating story: Masako Wakamiya, a Japanese woman, decided to learn how to develop mobile apps and successfully released her app. Guess her age? 82 years old! she created a game for older people. She was aware that many elderly people hate playing games as they were not designed for them, despite the benefits of keeping the brain active in older age.

"As you age, you lose many things: your husband, your job, your hair, your eyesight. The minuses are quite numerous. But when you learn something new, whether it be programming or the piano, it is a plus, it's motivating," - Masako Wakamiya.

Your computer or laptop won't get angry and say "Hey kid, don't try this" or "Old man, get out of here, you can't do it". It's all an illusion.

I don't deserve it

I can give you a list of more excuses, but the most important excuse is that you don't deserve to do this.

You might make excuses that you don't deserve this or other previously mentioned excuses.

There's good and bad news. If you want to undertake something significant, the voice in your head will tell you that you don't deserve to do it. You'll feel dumb, as though everyone else is better at it than you are and you possess no talent. If you hear such a voice and decide to search for another job, don't be shocked if the whisper comes back to haunt you.

This is an everyday situation that everyone goes through, so don't be worried. Because everything is easy at first, but the more serious you are and the longer you stay here, the more tough it will get. This is the point at which many people who give up easily will fail. For this reason, those that survive will be special.

We are more worried about outside voices, we are afraid of being looked down upon by others. We are afraid of being mocked by others, when all of that hasn't yet happened, we think of ourselves as incompetent. Everything happens in your head, you must realize that a negative internal voice always exists and it's a more dangerous foe than other individuals.

Not instant

If you've decided to dive into the world of coding, be prepared to encounter a variety of excuses, particularly those made by yourself. Even though you are initially excited, this does not guarantee that things will go smoothly. Encountering constraints are common, just keep going and continue to learn little by little.

"Most people overestimate what they can do in a day, and underestimate what they can do in a month. We overestimate what we can do in a year, and underestimate what we can accomplish in a decade."

Do what you can today, don't be afraid. Mastering skills is like climbing a high mountain.

After climbing inch by inch every day, you will eventually reach the summit.

We often condemn ourselves for our inability to learn something quickly. There is one minor issue: we instantly consider ourselves unworthy. Stop tormenting yourself! nothing is instant, people in movies look fantastic, the movie is just 2 hours long at most, and you think you can be an expert after watching a movie or reading a book. Unfortunately, this is not the case, in the real world, each of us must struggle and go through a lengthy process.

Don't be afraid of errors in your program. The longer you code, the more issues you may experience. When I face errors, I often feel discouraged and want to give up. But you know what happens every time? You will find the solution as long as you are willing to face and accept the error! You'll get past it eventually. You simply need to sit for a bit longer.

We all have no idea what we're doing and are still learning every day.

Get out of the tutorial circle

In addition to having studied in college, I attempted to find a program language teacher on YouTube at the beginning of the learning period. I took notes as needed and watched the video repeatedly when the material wasn't clear. As indicated in another section, There are many ways to learn programming, however, there are many traps that you may fall into.

It's OK to learn through watching video tutorials or reading how-to articles. But keep in mind, don't use it as a means of concealment when you keep browsing for tutorials because you're nervous to start working.

I haven't stopped learning, and the only way that I feel productive these days is to create something so that the lesson may be properly comprehended. It doesn't matter what I make, what matters is that I put what I've just learned into practice.

Have you ever tried to understand a concept using a video or how-to article, but it is hard to grasp? You can also use the methods described above, and try to put into practice what you've learned. You might be able to comprehend it better if you modify it with your code.

Begin practicing as soon as you learn something new. Open your text editor and retype what's on the screen. However, by learning to code from scratch, you can learn more from encountering errors in any system that does not function properly,

Tutorial videos or textbooks don't make you smart. They are similar to the fuel in your car, if you don't use it, it's useless.

I would suggest that you read a lot, including other people's code. Just like reading a sports book, you can't get good at sports just by reading the book, you must exercise. The same is true for coding, you must write your code.

Blank text editor

Starting a new project always has two sides: the passionate side of wanting to work on something and the bewildered side of not knowing where to begin. Opening a blank text editor can be daunting for programmers, and there are numerous excuses not to begin coding, just like a writer who finds himself faced with blank paper or a painter who is afraid to scratch his canvas.

Programmers have the same issue as other artists, who typically put off their jobs. We prefer to find reasons to put it off, even if they are favorable, such as having to think longer or ensure that it works. But it won't work unless you start coding.

If you are reluctant to write a program because you are frightened it will fail. There's good news: your task at first is to do a lot of lousy work! So don't be concerned about your work being subpar.

This is your job! Why? Because typically, good work can only come out after we've released all of the bad work.

Imagine your good work is currently clogged in a pipe, and you must remove the blocking items one by one until your good work emerges. Work a lot, even if you think it's mediocre work, that's just the way it is.

The code you write cannot and will never be flawless. As a human being who continually keeps learning, you will mature and realize that your previous work was not the best, but it was the best at the time. Now, put forth your best effort and make the best use of your time to begin developing the program.

People regret not doing what they should do more than they regret not achieving.

Beta Version

In the world of software, there is the term beta version. A beta version is one in which your application is not yet ready for use. Users wishing to try the beta version are already expecting errors to be discovered. There's also an alpha version, which is an early version of a program and is only tested by a small group of people.

Think about your program in this way: there is an alpha version and a beta version. You must accept that there may be errors and that the program is not flawless, therefore there is no need to be paranoid or to feel pressured that your program must run smoothly.

Many programmers are hesitant to begin writing code because they are concerned that their program will be poor. The project you are working on isn't horrible; it's just in beta at the moment.

The beautiful thing about your work is that you can always enhance it. If it's only a 6, that's okay, you may go back and attempt again to enhance it to a 10.

Editor mode is off

Pay close attention to the next paragraph if you find it hard to get things done because you always have the feeling that your work isn't perfect or you're terrified of failing.

When developing a program, you play two roles. The first one is a "Writer", and the second one is an "editor". Your responsibility as a program writer is to finish the program, it doesn't matter if it's ineffective, what matters is that it works the way you want it to. Shortly after, you may begin working as an "editor". This is where you play the role of an individual who improves your code to make it more user-friendly.

When you try to be both at the same time, you'll find hard to complete tasks because you'll constantly be criticizing yourself while working.

Allow yourself to make mistakes as a writer, and you can fix them as an editor.

Being scared is normal

We constantly shift from being terrified of one thing to another. We were terrified of ghosts, shots, and failing to make the grade when we were kids. Our worries change as we grow older, but if you're still reading this, it means you're still alive, still able to sleep at night, and still able to eat when you wake up.

More importantly, we can still think, learn, and do things to keep this life adventure going. All of your early anxieties are no longer relevant.

Unlike when we were kids, we're now terrified of failing when we set up a business, of being rejected when we apply for a job (or propose to a woman), or of receiving low grades in college.

We will overcome all of our fears. We are not alone in feeling this way, and we will face more than one fear. These concerns, believe it or not, are not as frightening as we assume.

We are hesitant to do anything even though we truly want to do it, we want to improve our surroundings, we want to contribute to great things, and we don't want to be average. But we're afraid of what people will say, what will happen after that, and what will happen if we fail, despite the fact that nothing happened yet.

The worst that can happen when we try something new is that our plan does not go as planned. Interesting fact: if we don't dare to do something and remain still now, our plan will fail because we don't do anything. As a result, reconsider what the difference is, the current situation in which our intentions have not been realized, and what the damage is in attempting. In fact, the second alternative remains the most likely.

In the past, I was terrified of settling on a major and a career path. Even while I was starting to code, there were so many options that I was frightened of taking the incorrect step or learning the wrong thing.

I would not have received the knowledge I have now if I had remained fearful at the time. Despite my fears, I continued to learn and make decisions, even if some of my decisions were wrong and not all of my knowledge was put to use, they all contributed to who I am today.

I was unsure about what career to pursue, but I enjoy sharing and want my work to benefit others. At the time, I decided to record everything that I knew and put it on YouTube due to having few decent programming manuals, despite the fact that this skill is incredibly vital nowadays. Unfortunately, I was afraid of responses from others and of being mocked.

I would like to offer valuable and applicable knowledge to people from all backgrounds. I would like to share my thoughts through podcasts and blogs. However, I was worried that no one would listen to the podcast or read the blog.

Despite my fear, I continued to type on the computer. I didn't sit around waiting for a publisher or an established figure to introduce me. Without anyone's permission, I began writing.

The risks were not as terrifying as I had thought, and my fear was unfounded. The point of this story is not about me, but about you! Fear does not distinguish us, it distinguishes us if we remain persistent.

Now is the time for you to do what you want, to engage in positive activities that can benefit others. Some fears will emerge. The solution is not to do nothing, but to act, fear will pass, and nothing is as frightening as we think.

We are primarily fearful observers who remain silent about the issue, fear being disregarded while proposing solutions, fear not using the product manufactured, and fear others disagreeing with our viewpoints.

What is the point? Not everyone will agree with us, not everyone will like us, and not everything we try will work, but we don't need all of that. We don't need everyone's approval, and we don't need all of our efforts to be successful. What we need to do is give our all to what we believe in.

Commenting on people's work is far easier than creating something, but the delight and advantages are enjoyed by the actor, not the commenter.

We have no control over the outcome, all we can do is try and pray. Inaction is the greatest risk of all.

Localhost is secure

Localhost refers to the server where you build your program in your computer. When just you and your code are aware of what you're creating. Nobody else will object or criticize.

Localhost is a safe haven, you can build a lot of things here, including beta versions to develop. However, there comes a time when you have to put your work out there.

You must leave localhost in order to receive critiques and feedback. Publicize your work and solicit feedback and critique. You don't have to pay for unfavorable feedback, so don't be afraid of it. You won't find out what has to be fixed if the program is simply saved on your computer server.

Share your work in community groups, social media, or other areas where other people can see it. Don't take negative feedback personally, you are already remarkable if you dare to create, let alone share and accept advice. Remember that you are still developing... The current you is incomplete.

It's a fact that most people won't care what you make, so acquiring feedback is beneficial. If you are afraid of criticism, there is a Mexican saying that says:

"They tried to bury us. They didn't know we were seeds."

This means that in order for a seed to grow into a mighty tree, it must first be planted or buried; consider harsh criticism to be your means to be planted.

When you venture outside of localhost, however, there are numerous opportunities. You'll meet people who share your enthusiasm for what you're creating, or a corporation may see your work and want to hire you.

Many open-source project creators have also obtained financial resources, job opportunities, and assistance from others.

All because he had the guts to leave localhost and share what he had. Show the world your work!

Learn in public

Killing two birds with one stone. Why not create a program while you learn?

This learning method is highly unique, and few people seek to learn new things in public places. It does not imply reading a book in the middle of the street, but rather making use of the internet to share what you have learned. This can benefit both others and yourself. As long as the platform is available to a large number of users, the approach can include writing blogs, posting on social media, making films, talking in communities, and other cyberspace activities.

How can you assist yourself in this manner? The internet is a big, limitless space. When you're learning something new, many other people have already learned it, and they know where you're going to struggle. Others have the opportunity to criticize, in this case, good criticism, what you may have misinterpreted or if there is a better approach to finish the task by leaving yourself available.

You can develop a blog that is detectable by search engines, so that when a user searches for the same reference, they can reach your blog. You can also discuss your troubles on social media or ask directly on community forums, and more seasoned experts are coming to help you.

Write code in public

As programmers, we must not only learn the theory but also write the program. Therefore, you can practice the process of learning in public by creating code.

When you have sufficient skills, you can begin contributing to open source projects. Don't be afraid to make mistakes, the project manager always thoroughly review your code. If the code is required, it will be included in the system. If not, it won't matter. Your good intentions to contribute would be appreciated.

Beginning to develop your own tool (package, plugin, or framework) for public consumption will educate you a lot. Because it will be read by a large number of people, you will tend to write it neatly, perhaps to avoid being perceived as unattractive and to make it easier for others to read.

Begin by developing a software you require, you may need to add features to or remove an error from an existing program.

It is beneficial to begin by fixing your problems. You know what to do and what kind of outcome you desire.

Putting your code in a public server is unsettling, but it's a demanding task with numerous benefits. It's possible that the code you supplied is required by another person.

You can learn while writing code and assisting others.

Which tool is the best

Seth Godin, an American writer and marketer, told a fictional story in which Harry Potter author, JK Rowling held a press conference and a journalist asked, *"Your writing is amazing, what pencil do you use to write?"*

What do you think about that person's query? Is it significant or not? Of all, the fact that the Harry Potter series of novels has made her one of the richest authors is not due to the fine pencils she uses, but to the popularity of the novels.

We are likely to get stuck not to start the project because we believe our current tools are inadequate or want to find out tools used by the experts. We overlook the fact that the work is more essential than the tools.

Start writing code and you'll find out whether the tool fits you or whether you need to do further research.

I'll give you advice on selecting a tool, programming language, library, or framework to work:

- Consider its popularity. A tool is often popular because many programmers find it useful. You may see quantitative indicators, such as the number of stars a project has on github or the number of followers it has on social media. Indeed, this isn't everything, there are exciting new technologies that people are unaware of.
- When was the last time it was modified? As technology advances, particular frameworks or libraries can no longer be used because parts of their code no longer support specific tools or browsers. As a result, it's critical to determine whether it's still being actively developed or has been abandoned.
- Consider the issues. On github, there is a 'issues' section where you can see a list of issues with the code; if you see that it is

neglected and there are a lot of serious ones, it might not be the right tool for you.

Regardless of these tips, you know best of which tool to choose. If you're merely working on a beta or prototype, I'd recommend using a tool that you're familiar with so you can get feedback quickly.

If you already know you're going to produce something big and extensive, you can undertake more in-depth study to determine which tools are best for you. Don't be afraid to seek advice from those with prior experience.

You only have to be cautious since not all viewpoints are heard. In this regard, when comparing a programming language or framework, people often declare framework A is faster, despite merely a 'hello world' message. You may require more than such a program.

Get Money From Code

Knocking on the door of opportunity

What happens after you've learned? Normally, we wish to make money from our favorite hobby. There are numerous opportunities for employment across the country, and the demand for technical talent, particularly programmers, is growing as businesses expand.

Unfortunately, for those of you who have recently completed your studies, this door appears to be closed, and you feel unqualified due to your lack of experience. "To work, you need experience, to have experience, you need to work," as if you were wondering which came first, the egg or the chicken.

While the door is still closed, you can begin knocking on it in the hopes that someone will open it, or you can eventually open the door yourself.

1T Project

Not one thousand dollars, but "**Thanks**, dude!" This phrase is used when you do the job but are not compensated financially, "only" with thanks.

Do you have to do the work for free?

You are not required to do so, but many of us do so because we have not built a project that demonstrates that we have mastered such an expertise. Employers need solid evidence to see your work experience and expertise. For this reason, employers make offers to programmers to do programming jobs.

It may be an offer from a friend or family member, they may have a small business that requires a website or app. By assisting them, you can acquire knowledge and expertise from doing real work, despite not being compensated.

Why not earn money while also assisting them? Despite their small business, try to make an offer, "I charge for this amount, what do you think?" If the worst-case scenario is "no," you can do the job for free, as its initial intent, you haven't lost anything.

Internship at the company

You can enter an office environment or a start-up company without qualifying as an employee to take the next step into the actual world of work. Companies typically offer internships for college students or amateurs.

Although the work may not be what you expected, being in a real environment will motivate you to enter this world. Not to mention the possibility to meet people who are already working in the sector on a daily basis. You get the ability to speak personally and ask many of your questions.

I have a tip, despite not many companies advertise open internship opportunities, don't hesitate to offer yourself. Try sending an email or bringing your CV directly to the company, and tell them honestly and politely what you expect and what you can do for them. Take the initiative rather than just wait.

Make a project with buddies or by yourself

Another alternative is to work on a project alone or with buddies. You have the same potential to build a product as everyone else. Remember that as programmers, we have the advantage of starting research at a lower cost than other companies.

As a result, start creating products and projects that will drive you to get out of bed every day. You can do a large task in stages.

There is no need to expect millions of users to use the product because you will benefit from it.

Sign up for a bootcamp or talent scouting company

Talent scouting companies, bootcamps or training programs related to coding, typically have agreements with multiple companies ready to enable you to start working.

Such companies never stop looking for new employees, particularly those that are enthusiastic about their profession. The benefit is that they already aware what qualities they are looking for, so you can consult and follow the specific learning program, if provided. They also have contacts with companies looking to hire you.

Expanding the network

Have you ever heard the term 'the power of an insider'? There are two interpretations. The first one has a negative interpretation, in which you lack the qualities that the organization seeks yet a prominent insider insists on hiring you. The second one has a positive interpretation, when a trustworthy employee in the company recommends you because they know exactly what the company's needs are that match your abilities.

Try to get involved in online forums or real-world communities. In addition to the many benefits of community that we have previously discussed, you can be recognized by many other people who may already be working in a company and are seeking an individual to hire.

You can take the following actions:

- Find forums on the internet and participate in discussions (assist others).
- Throw productive arguments or crucial inquiries (not necessarily technical topics) in online forums.
- Attend community events, introduce yourself, and get to know each other.
- Don't just be a participant, attempt to join the board.

By broadening your network, you increase your chances for finding suitable employment.

Degrees and Certificates

Paypal Mafia is group of former PayPal employees and founders (an online payment company) who moved on to other projects in technology, such as Elon Musk, the founder of Tesla and SpaceX, Chad Hurley, the co-founder of YouTube, Reid Hoffman, the co-founder of Linkedin. Among the many well-known figures is Peter Thiel, one of the early investors in the largest social media platform, Facebook.

Peter Thiel's controversial opinions are expressed in his book, Zero to One, one of the role model books for company entrepreneurs. No less intriguing, he has a scholarship program, but not to pay for someone to go to college, rather, he has a program known as the Thiel Fellowship, which gives $100,000 to young people who choose to leave or not go to college to build new things.

He is not the only person to have an extreme opinion about college, take a look at Steve Jobs (the founder of Apple) and Mark Zuckerberg (the founder of Facebook), both of whom voluntarily dropped out of college. In order to achieve what they had always believed. Don't be gloomy if you don't have a degree or certificate.

Seek Validation From Others

It is common for people to pay for a certificate or a degree without having any prior knowledge of the subject matter.

In the world of knowledge seekers, there is one extremely crucial component that is often overlooked: acquiring knowledge and being able to put it in the real world.

We hold the view that the government has created an ideal system, with stages ranging from elementary school to college, and numerous jobs waiting for you since you have an additional degree behind your name. Unfortunately, it is not how the actual world works. It is a hard pill to swallow.

Gradually, the business realized that excellent grades alone are not sufficient to propel a company forward. Competing with a variety of emerging companies powered by creative individuals requires bright ideas and real skills that may be used to grow their companies.

Degrees and certificates are simply byproducts of following a system developed and designed by others. They are not evidence that you can create a product that you've always desired.

Needless to say, a company or college can develop a better system to issue certifications solely to those who truly grasp the subject matter.

Collecting portfolio

All of these things, whether it's a 1T project, an internship, or your project, can be included in a portfolio.

Don't just offer a title or the image of your product, you must make thorough documentation. Write a detailed description of what you did, what you learned, and how you can improve. This demonstrates that you are an individual who is constantly learning new things and is aware of your own flaws.

You can add this list to your CV (work history) when looking for a job, so that others can see that you have done a lot of real work rather than merely passively learning.

Where to keep the portfolio?

The internet is the best place to showcase your work. Most talent scouts might come across you there. You can upload your CV and past activities to job search sites, such as LinkedIn (and possibly more sites in the future).

You can put your code in a place where people can see the code you've written down to its roots, such as Github, Gitlab, Bitbucket, or other sites. They typically want to see more details about your skills in coding.

Another critical aspect is to create a personal webpage. You can utilize simple programs like WordPress, or if you want to express yourself effectively, you can learn to create your own website.

You don't have to pick just one, you can submit your work to as many different sources as you like. The advantage of having a personal website is that you have complete control. While other sites may change their algorithms, the way they work, or may one day be shut down, you still have a backup to manage - your personal site.

Your work, your choice

When most people used horses to transport goods, Henry Ford invented a machine that could do what we now call a car. Not only that, he was well-known for inventing a process for mass production in his plant.

Despite all of his accomplishments, which changed the world of the automotive industry and made him wealthy, he reminded businessmen that *"a business that makes nothing but money is a poor business."*

Starting from the end

There are many careers available if you solely consider money. But, can money alone make your life complete? How many wealthy and successful people have opted for ending their lives?

Don't choose a job just for the money, there's a lot you can gain that isn't always financial. With the power of programming, there are so many lives you can help and problems you can solve.

Choose your area of interest, and you can start at the end, by looking for companies engaged in solving these problems. You can apply for jobs at companies with the same vision and mission as you.

Be responsible with your code. Many people may benefit from the lines of your code. Choose wisely, what areas of the problem do you want to help, and what motivates you to wake up in the morning and get to work. Many people complained on their social media, "Another Monday!... sigh".

On the other hand, if you choose the wrong job, you will be responsible for the suffering of many people. You will be responsible for the suffering of many people when you are working in companies that harm health, such as cigarette companies, or companies that harm the mind, such as porn sites. The better your job, the more negative impact on others. Take responsibility for your code.

Your mentality will be significantly different, when you're merely working, odds are you'll come up with an improvised approach to achieve things, and almost every day turns into a hardship. On the other, when you are passionate about what you do, doing your best is always a choice, and you will have a positive feeling because you are contributing to something you value.

Job vacancies as curriculum

By being job specific, you can find out employment opportunities of companies and take note of the qualifications required. You can then include these qualifications in your learning curriculum.

You're more likely to be the person they're seeking for if you learn in a directed manner. Make a captivating resume, they receive hundreds of resumes every day. What makes you distinctive, what qualifies you for this position?

Tell them you're interested in what they're doing, tell them about the activities that you do outside of coding to demonstrate your interest in the issue, and tell them about how you've been learning, specifically to help their company, because you've turned the qualification into a learning curriculum.

Combining your mind, physical activity and heart is no easy feat, but when you manage to bring them together, the sky's the limit!

Finding a job will be exhausting

Just because you're excited to work, it doesn't mean everything will be simple. The job-hunting process can be exhausting. You must accept that some companies will reject you.

If you are rejected by the companies, don't get discouraged. Rejection is common. There's no need to freak out and become inferior.

Increase your confidence. When you have confidence, you will be more willing to knock on a number of doors, leading to more opportunities.

Back up your confidence with continuous learning and skill development. Demonstrate that you are qualified for the position and that you can contribute positively to the organization.

You do not have to meet all of the requirements listed in the job vacancies. Employers will appreciate your efforts if you're honest about what you're good at, your weaknesses, and your endeavors to overcome your weaknesses.

However, it does not guarantee that you will be hired. Accepting an employee involves numerous factors, including culture fit, talents, work experience, and whether there are better applicants available at the time. You have no control over whether or not you will be hired, but you can manage your effort.

Maximizing Effort

You can maximize your job hunt efforts by carrying out the following:

- Create a professional CV (many experts explain how to create a decent CV in general).
- Write a motivation letter. It should explain why you want to work and what you can contribute.
- Both should be read several times. Don't directly send them following their completion. Take your time reading the CV and letter. Is there any incorrect punctuation? Are there any

unclear sentences? Make them "perfect" in every way.

- Prepare a portfolio, proof of your work over the years.
- Don't hesitate to consult with experts. Not only are many individuals sharing ideas and tricks on the internet, but you can also ask others you are acquainted with (in person or on social media) for more.
- When an application appears appealing, you will be invited to an interview. Prepare yourself well.
- Begin practicing to avoid being nervous. When you get nervous, things you say may differ from what you are thinking.
- Basic questions such as self-introduction, what you do, why you want to work here, what you've accomplished, and how much you want to be paid (if not previously specified) should have your responses ready.

Creating a resume, writing a motivation letter, and conquering the interview require expertise that cannot be covered in this book. Take it easy, you have a friend named "the internet" to help you.

Twists and turns of the job

Unlike in the past, when working meant dressing up, leaving in the morning, and returning home in the evening, today's work is more diversified, with numerous different means of working to accommodate our increasingly dynamic and globally connected lives.

Full-time or freelance

The freelancer community is growing, because demands in a company can be met in a short period of time without the need to recruit personnel full-time. The companies recognize that there is no need to pay a salary every month if the work can be completed within the specified time frame.

Freelancing implies that you are not bound to a corporation, you make a contract within a specific time frame and execute the allocated tasks. This type of work is suitable for people who are easily bored, can manage their time well, despise feeling restricted, and are unconcerned about uncertainty.

Freelance does not mean free without any limitations, you need to meet the satisfactory standards desired by the project provider, therefore, intensive communication is needed, especially when you don't work at the company, it takes extra effort to get to know them better and find out the objective of the project.

If you do a good job, they may refer you to others, or you may be contacted for the following project.

A company provides benefits when you work on a permanent basis. Apart from the salary for employees to live comfortably, companies also provide other benefits, such as insurance, allowance, and various other benefits depending on the employer.

As mentioned in the previous section, choose your employment carefully, particularly if you are permanent employees. You will be spending a lot of time here, so consider what sort of culture they have, what facilities you require, how big the team is, and numerous other considerations. When looking for a job, read the company profile as well as the qualifications.

Another benefit of permanent workers is that you will most likely have a career or a promotion as your contribution grows. In this case, a junior developer may advance to senior status, then manager, CTO, and so on. Your job will not be monotonous, you are required to be more creative as your position advances.

What about freelancing? Does this mean that your job is boring? There is the word free in freelancing; yet, if you execute a monotonous task, you may become bored. As a freelancer, you get to choose your next challenge.

Remote or on-site

When you visit employment sites, you may find a filter called remote indicating that you can work from anywhere, including your home, without having to go to the office.

With the internet reaching practically every place and a unifying language (we use English in global domain), it is not impossible to hire people from all across the globe.

Companies known for remote working include WordPress (a website to make it easy for users to create blogs), Basecamp (a project management website), and X-team (a website that connects programmers wishing to work remotely with suitable projects).

Remote working differs, some demand you to come to the office on occasion, others want you to be in the same time zone so you may work at a specific hour, and yet others are fully free, allowing you to manage your schedule.

Remote work does not allow you to be lazy because no one is looking; in fact, when you fail to stay on schedule with time, work might be neglected and you jeopardize other people's businesses. To work remotely, you must have particular additional talents, such as the ability to work autonomously, as well as good time management and comprehensive communication.

Some people are not suited to remote work, they prefer coming to the workplace and having a working environment, as well as being able to meet with friends and connect directly.

Migrate

If the company you desire isn't in your place of residence and you'd prefer to work on the spot, you can migrate. Many of the people I know have chosen to relocate to the capital in order to pursue their desired careers, particularly if they live in a location where there aren't many work opportunities in the tech industry.

Being in a new environment can be unsettling but it may bring benefits. You can learn about a different culture, live dynamically or flexibly, and become independent.

Ideally, you wish to develop your region, but you have to be like an arrow that needs to be tugged a bit before it can move quickly. You must make a number of sacrifices in order to achieve your dreams, including leaving your hometown.

I continually encourage those who migrate to return and share what they've learned.

Words can be forgotten

Learn to be professional in any line of employment you choose, whether it's freelance or aiding others. It's not just in what you accomplish, but also in how you interact with others.

People are eager to do anything, including torture themselves, simply due to a new job. It's fairly uncommon to hear complaints that a person's job is stressful, that they have to stay up late, that clients want more features than promised, that family members need aid when they have other tasks to perform, and a variety of other issues may arise.

Words can be forgotten, and what you commit to in the beginning may change significantly in practice. For this reason, you need a written record, known as a contract. This document summarizes what you agreed upon at the beginning, what you wish to make, and how long you expect it to take to complete.

Even if you're new to this, there are numerous advantages to doing so. There is no more "please add ABC features" or "I want you to have it done tomorrow" because all the agreements have been included in the contract. All you have to do is tell the person to whom you're selling your services, "I will complete the features and meet the deadline". Additional fees may apply to the additional tasks.

When you have a job on the go, keep in mind that you must be completely dedicated to it. If you can't complete it, don't just say yes to the next request for assistance or extra chores. Tell your schedule, I work from this time to this time and can only accept new tasks till X date. If you're hesitant to say no, you can accumulate a lot of work, which ends up costing everyone.

Your concentration wanes, your time becomes disorganized, and your tasks are neglected. Be extremely cautious before adding more tasks.

Purple cow

Imagine you're driving home and come across a herd of cows looking for grass, these cows are brown, like most cows, you might turn around a little, but the vehicle keeps moving. What would you do if these cows were purple and had a distinctive pattern? You will come to a complete stop to enjoy the color and begin photographing this moment.

The concept of the "purple cow" is defined by Seth Godin in his book of the same name, one of the books that I find it impossible not to talk about and suggest to others.

What gets the adrenaline running in the second cow troupe and makes you want to stop? They're unique, they're not monotonous, and they're not afraid to try something new.

I'm not talking about cows; I'm talking about you. What happens when people come to know you? Is it boring or intriguing to them? For the latter, you must be a purple cow, presenting something different from what has already been seen.

Because the world of technology is so vast, you may be able to stand out from the crowd with your unique skills. Perhaps you want to investigate machine learning, develop a product for the Internet of Things (IoT), investigate website accessibility, or something else. Dig deeper than anyone else, learn on a consistent basis, and share what you learn. It's referred to as being a specialist.

Combining two or more diverse abilities is not impractical. For example, if you're good at making videos, why not start a video channel where you can share what you've learned? If you enjoy the culinary world, which is unrelated to technology, you can combine these two different things into something new, a purple cow. You might be able to use artificial intelligence to create a recipe website or a sophisticated machine that can analyze food ingredients and then recommend a specific menu. Feel free to express your wildest ideas.

When applying for a job, hobbies and work experience will make job seekers feel like they are walking back home and stumbled upon a purple cow. They won't miss it. In comparison, if you're like the rest of the applicants, you'll be heaped up with the others to be sent to the barn.

Create your own business

God gives unlimited fortune. Other than earning money through salaries paid by others, you also have the same opportunity to create a business to earn money.

A merchant adorned his cart with the words "God is incomparably rich, how can I fear poverty?"

There's so much to talk about in the business world that it would take a book to cover it all, but there's actually only one thing you need... to get started.

Make the one you want

Is there an app or tool you wish existed in the world but no one has created it yet? Why not strive to be the first? Is there an app that irritates you because a feature should be introduced or something should be improved? Why don't you give it a shot?

Maya Angelou, an American writer, states that if you don't like something, change it. If you can't change it, change your attitude. Don't complain. Rather than complaining about what you're going through, consider earning money from such circumstances.

You know the end outcome you want to accomplish by starting with what you enjoy doing. This can facilitate you to expand your project and helps you stay motivated on a regular basis. You and others' complain can serve as the basis for a project. It doesn't have to be something big.

Grab, an Malaysian startup, began as a motorcycle taxi before expanding its services throughout the country. Similarly, Google began as a search engine and Facebook was only used on one campus. Setting a specified area or target market can be advantageous. You can determine whether your idea is needed by the community before embarking on a larger endeavor that requires further funding.

Is it possible to establish your own company?

Your current objective is not to establish an enterprise! You have the wrong focus. You can learn marketing, finance, or recruiting later on. Your current focus is on creating a product that consumers are willing to pay for. I'm sure if I'd known what to learn to start a business, I wouldn't have started my business with such little knowledge.

This is the key. You can do it yourself. It has its own community called Indie Hacker, not one that breaks into the system as you watched on the media. Indie Hacker is individuals who attempt, perform an experiment, and establish their own business (albeit they are not truly alone because they have the internet, peers, and a community to learn from).

Being among other people is beneficial, you can begin with a person you already know and trust. If you already have a playmate, why not start looking for a companion with whom you can make money? Isn't it more fun if you both succeed?

It is best to choose buddies with diverse abilities so that you can complement each other. Moreover, if you can find partners who are experts in the sector whose issues you wish to solve.

For instance, if you wish to create a culinary product, collaborating with a chef or an individual with a nutrition background will be beneficial. Another example: if you want to create an app for bikers, having an avid cyclist will assist you define the product, instead of starting with an idea, which is not always needed.

Where does the money come from?

In some situations, you may require money at the outset, there are numerous ways to earn money, but the first step is to begin with a little amount of capital. You can work on the weekdays and create your project on the weekends.

Alternatively, you can earn money from side hustles. You can either start your own agency and get clients or continue working for a company. You use the money as startup capital for your company.

Second, you can seek finance from relatives or close friends, either as a loan or as an investment in the form of shares if your business is successful. It is critical to explore this thoroughly because it can be destructive to relationships.

Third, find an investor. Angel investor or VC (venture capital) is a word used in the startup business. This is where a person, group of people, or company looks for digital businesses to invest in exchange for shares.

Fourth, I've heard of people taking part in hackathons, a competition held to finish certain programming issues within a few days and win rewards. This prize money is then used as capital.

Other sources of financing include government funding, participation in business incubation, and others. One thing is for sure: you must exercise caution, keep in mind that you are planning to create a product, not wasting time asking for money.

Level Up

Just getting started

We're all just getting started, and it's still a long road ahead of us. You are still in beta, and there is always something that can be improved as long as you are willing to adjust.

This is only level one
This is only practice
This is only the beginning

There are numerous next levels
There are many monsters to be found there
There are abilities to be mastered
There are several new weapons to be used

The more you walk, the more difficult it becomes. You don't expect to get here, and the next challenges seems impossible to achieve, yet you keep going.

Get ready to go to the next level.

Who's afraid error?

You were terrified of errors, but now it's time to look for them! As a programmer, it is critical to be prepared for all potential errors from the beginning in order to reduce the number of errors spotted by users of the programs.

You wouldn't like users to abandon your app because of an error you could have avoided. While everyone else is hiding to avoid bugs, you're picking up your sword and going out to find these monsters.

Write down numerous scenarios of how your app will be used. You can employ regular people (possible users) to test it out and discover where they struggle and where problems arise. This is known as usability testing.

Logging Bugs

Keeping track of the errors and fixing them has saved me many times when working with bugs. Surely, you don't want to waste time looking for the same solution. Document the bugs and how do you fix them.

The following are effective techniques to document a bug the first time you encounter it:

- Write down where, when, and on what device (browser / device) you found the error.
- What you expect or assume should occur
- How you and the team reproduce the bug
- Make a note of any speculations about the cause as a first hint.

Don't just use

Before I begin learning how to utilize a tool (application, library, framework, or programming language), I prefer to find out who created it. I'll hunt for articles, movies, or podcasts that explain why they created this product. Aside from what they say, I will learn a lot about how they think and their passion for problem solving.

Go programming language was created because there had been no significant improvements in programming languages over the years, while its hardware continued to improve, the Go language developers can see things that have not been completely utilized. Furthermore, in the beginning of PHP, Rasmus Lerdorf required Go language to build a website since the available language was too difficult for repetitive work.

We'll find a common thread among these inventors: they desire to fix their problem or satisfy their curiosity. Therefore, if you have a problem or are inquisitive about something, don't keep it to yourself because it could potentially fix many other people's problems.

Reading documentation

Many inexperienced programmers are too indolent to read. They want answers to their questions as soon as possible. If they had been a bit more patient and read a little more, their problems could have had more meaningful solutions.

Read the documentation for the tools you use. Almost all of your questions have previously been answered, along with case studies.

Another factor that contributes to a tool's popularity is that it keeps documentation neat and easy to read. If you don't learn a tool well, you won't be able to use it to its maximum potential. "If you only know a hammer, you'll see everything as a nail," as the adage goes.

The code contents and how the tool's author develops the code should be reviewed on a regular basis. Something we believed was miraculous turns out to be something we can easily create. Looking for the root cause of why this may happen is analogous to looking for gold, only that what you will find is tremendous knowledge.

The more you learn about a tool, the more incredible the things you can do with it. Don't be readily persuaded that tool A is superior to tool B. People who argue without reasoning get to the misleading conclusion.

We could be losing out on an incredible tool that could help us get our work done just because we read a post that claims 'tool A is not functioning, despite the fact that the author hasn't done a thorough investigation.

Don't believe everything you hear; do your own research!

Think deeper

When we want to do anything, we all think about it. But... some people think lightly, while others ponder deeply. Attempting to think deeper is referred to as critical thinking. It is a period when we can honestly query something even if we don't know the answer or our knowledge is inaccurate.

Thinking deeper is the fundamental capital for excelling beyond others. Although most people simply observe what is in front of them, thinking people may plan beyond that. Not only can we see further ahead, but critical thinking can also cause us to withdraw and reflect more deeply on our actions.

What are the benefits for programmers?

The longer you develop a program, particularly the same one, your mind no longer work harder, your mind can process almost everything effortlessly. You feel like you have an amazing skill and can do things faster, but you're also resting your mind.

Putting your mind at rest is critical. This implies that if you initially thought this was a creative profession, you will eventually find it uninteresting because your work no longer challenges you.

One day, you wrote a program when, without thinking, it worked. You wrote the next function, and it also worked. Until a few days later, when you added a new feature and all of a sudden.... an error occurred when running the program. Despite numerous attempts to fix the error, it remained troublesome. You have no idea why the error occurred because you did not know how it worked.

- *adapted from the Pragmatic Programming*

If you just "get it to work" when writing a program code, you will run into errors. You must consider whether this is the most efficient method, whether there is a risk of errors if the user does a wrong input, whether the program is using too much memory, and other negative possibilities.

Coding is simply a minor component of the process

If you think of coding as simply writing programs, you're mistaken. Long before that, we must plan what we intend to create, including architecture, database structure, language or framework, and so on. The more serious you are about this programming area, the more you must think about the technical system that will be put in place. All of this requires consideration.

Having an understanding of your application and how it will be utilized requires planning from the very beginning. We often adopt other developers' database structures or architecture, though the case at hand is distinct. Determine your specific needs and proceed.

Inquire further

When you want to do anything in your daily life, try asking yourself. Is anything you want to do important, and will it benefit you?

It could be knowledge, money, or anything else. Consider whether a job will be beneficial or detrimental to others before taking it.

If you get a job from a client to create "Project A." As a typical worker, you instantly accept the job and begin creating the requested system. After some time, it becomes clear that "Project A" is not what the client wants.

By thinking critically, when a client comes to you with task "A," you will think, question yourself, and ask the client what they truly want, and then you will try to explain whether or not this task of making "A" can help them. Before wasting a lot of time and money. You also give additional options that are more appropriate for their needs, not just "A," but other tasks that you can also perform.

This does not only apply between you and a client, it may be a startup you wish to launch or working in an office and receiving a task from your employer.

Not only before making a product, but also before creating a feature, you need to think more carefully. Before investing in anything, ask if it is important and if it is suited for purpose.

Experimenting like a scientist

Scientists conduct research to determine whether their hypothesis is correct or false. Despite the fact that they are certain about their hypothesis, it cannot be considered valid unless it has been proven.

Will Wright, a game designer for Electronic Arts Inc, says he learns more from games that seem amazing on paper (planned) but fail in the market. During a job interview, one of the inquiries is how many failed attempts he has made.

As a programmer whose work is linked to the internet, we get a lot of feedback online, on social media, or when we visit video-sharing sites or blogs. These factors might confuse our minds, causing us to misinterpret a notion just because we've heard it so many times.

When you have an opinion, learn like a scientist who conducts research, because it is highly possible that your opinion is incorrect.

Starting with prototypes (basic versions) of the things you want to verify, such as whether "xyz" technology is suitable for creating particular items, the cost of undertaking research is not as high as scientists who operate in laboratories. Make a basic version of what you're working on and test this "xyz" technology to see if it meets your needs.

You can ask professionals or study their documentation on the internet, but we often learn things without the proper context, so inquire with your problem in mind. What we intend to build may differ from how the technology is implemented, thus we must sometimes prove things to ourselves.

Dare to experiment with new things. When you fail, you're not really failing, you're just going in the wrong direction. It's possible that your trial will lead to novel and unexplored ideas.

James Dyson, the inventor of the vacuum cleaner that has since earned him a fortune, spent 15 years of his life and nearly all of his savings to develop the vacuum cleaner. He has a message for you:

"We're taught to do things the right way. But if you want to discover something that other people haven't, you need to do things the wrong way. Initiate a failure by doing something that's very silly, unthinkable, naughty, dangerous.

Create a Product

Some businesses just require four working days. The other day, their employees are encouraged to try something new, so that they are not bored with time-consuming tasks.

Your tasks can be tedious if you already have a job. You may become rigid workers who used to enjoy exploring things with programs.

Therefore, schedule time for your side projects, not simply learning, but also creating something that interests you. You should customize it to your particular situation. If you have a family, you must communicate with them during this extra time.

Your side project activities provide motivation for you to improve your work.

Remember how wonderful coding was when you first found it. When your difficulty is solved, it can make you feel "Wow" and satisfied.

Keep making a project, it doesn't have to be completed in a single day. If your project is only completed on weekends and can only be completed for two hours per week, a spectacular product may be born if you continually work on it and keep developing it! At the very least, you've made good use of your leisure time.

Nothing lasts forever

Computers used to be very large. The size is shrinking all the time. Now, look at your current smartphone with incredible technology.

HISTORY OF **COMPUTERS**

When USB was all the rage, we could transfer data with this tiny device. We no longer require physical devices because data can now be saved in the cloud.

Everything will change, and what you learn now may become obsolete in the future. Be open to new experiences and never stop learning.

Always be a student who is open to learning from everywhere.

Finding out the principles of what you are studying, comprehending the fundamentals is far more important than its implementation.

The implementation may change, but the framework may remain the same. Don't just learn the literal. Learn what is not visible.

The framework may change, but the implementation may not. Don't only memorize the actual meaning. Discover what is hidden.

Learning one programming language can make learning new programming languages easier in the future.

As long as you understand the framework, learning to design a tool in language X can make it easier for you to create the same tool in language Y.

The app you're using right now might not be the same as the one you'll use at your prospective company or employment. It will be simple to make the transition as long as you understand the main concept of the program.

The future may not be what you think it will be. Your point of view could be incorrect. Learn to listen and continue to learn.

Nothing is constant, except change.

Fixing code

In *Pragmatic Programming* book, **Andy Hunt** and **David Thomas** say programming is like gardening. You need to make a plan, prepare soil, fertilizer, plants, and so on. Additionally, when the plant grows, something unexpected may happen, some plants may fail to grow or the yields are not be as expected. You need to take care of the plants again, remove weeds, move the plants, fertilize the soil, and many more.

If you think your code is bad, welcome! It is just the way we are as humans who are constantly learning. You may be very proud of what you made. However, when you look at it again, you want to improve a few things. This is a very positive thing because you are ready and willing to change for the better   every   day.

Reid Hoffman, LinkedIn co-founder and investor in several startups once said *"If you are not embarrassed by the first version of your product, you've launched too late."*

He said that the first version of whatever you create may be bad and embarrassing in retrospect, but it is a sign that you have the courage to put something out there without waiting for it to be perfect.

Unfinished

"You have completed the code, but your job isn't finished.

Take a look at a project you've been working on for a while, and take a peek at the code, how is it? do you feel like you didn't write it? Try rewriting the code, what would you like to improve? and how do you make it more efficient?

The process is called refactoring. Refactoring means organizing your code without modifying its original functionality. Refactoring is deliberately performed to maximize the code in order to run faster, be more efficient, and last but not least, easy to read by humans, including yourself.

Imagine you have ongoing projects. A few months or years later, due to an error, you are required to fix it... and when you open the code... what a nightmare! The code is messy and hard to understand. It ends up taking extra time to understand the code or you might have to start over from scratch.

Another example is when you're working with a team, if you don't have the intention to fix the code (it just works), your team may find it difficult to read and add new features, and it takes a long time to understand the code, this can hinder the growth of your product. A stunted product means a stunted business.

Elimination

Never be afraid to delete parts of your code. I often comment out (comment out means to disable lines of code in a program) parts of my code with the thought of "who knows if I'll need it later", but in the end, I didn't.

Keep your code clear of those cobwebs, if you're worried a function will be needed, store it somewhere else outside of your code, there are plenty of note-taking apps for such purposes, don't confuse yourself.

Don't be afraid to delete old code, you can always use git (version control system, discussed in the next section) to secure your code.

Easy to read by humans

One of the criteria for good code is easily readable by humans. It must be readable by other people other than yourself. You can do several things to make the code easier to read:

1. Good naming

Naming variables, functions, classes and all parts of your code should not be random. For example, don't just write x=3, but give a name to x, such as area=3. By doing this, people are aware that it's the area in the program.

Or you can write the name of a function, if you just write calculate() (to perform calculation) while there are many things to be calculated in your program, you may get frustrated. Change the name to be more specific, for example, to calculate the area, write calculateArea()

2. Functions should do only one thing

Each function should only do one thing according to its name. If you're creating a registration system. Don't pile up all the tasks in the same function: saving the user's data to the database, sending an email confirmation, or signing them up for the newsletter. Separate the functions into one distinct function.

3.Consistent format

Visually, your code affects the readers whether it is easy to read or not. Use a consistent format. For example, for naming variables or functions, you can choose whether to use camel case (example: nameCamelCase) or snake case (example: name_snake_case) or any other format as long as it is consistent.

Code indentation or spacing also affects visual efforts. Some programmers use tab or space. Tabs can be set at 2 or 4 spaces or whatever you set. With consistent indentation in each block, your code may look neat.

4.Comment only when necessary

Programmers often overuse comments. They comment on almost all functions or lines of code, which is unnecessary. Make your own code easy to read in the first place so that it no longer needs a comment. Only use comments when truly necessary.

You also need to read up on the best practices for writing in each language you use, as each language generally has the guidelines.

DRY: Don't Repeat Yourself

Look at your code, are there dynamic functions that can be created? are there blocks of code you write over and over again that can be made into the same function (DRY Don't Repeat Yourself)? or are there large sections of code that you can abstract away to make everything more organized and readable.

DRY is a popular mantra in programming since our goal is to make things automatic and non-repeatable, the same philosophy should be applied when writing the code, not repeating the same code over and over again.

—

Refactor your code gradually. Change the required code one by one, function by function, then test, then change the next code. Don't change multiple lines of code at once, you may find it difficult to fix errors that may not have been present before.

Writing a program is not for an instant. Just like writing a book, there is a writing mode (when you focus on writing only) and an editor mode (when you want to improve and review the writing).

Refactoring your code allows it to be easier to understand, easier to change, more efficient, and easier to find bugs.

You can be replaced

"The future programmer will know that the best thing he can do for his project is to be replaceable".
- **Yegor Bugayenko**.

Some might think negatively, "why do we want to be replaced so easily? Don't we want to work as long as possible?".

In addition to writing documentation of the code, writing clean and readable code allows your team or the next person to continue your project without problems. Thus, the project can be continued without any obstacles. When you are sick or there are obstacles, the project can still run, this is a very good thing for you to do.

Selfish people don't want to do that, because they want to feel important and needed. Unfortunately, you won't live forever or keep working in the same place. For this reason, you need to code and document the program from scratch so that someone else can continue the program.

"What will happen to you?" The fact that you are doing so means that you are a person who is ready to grow and doesn't like doing the same thing over and over again.

The next challenge will come, a better job will come. You will go up to the next level. Don't hesitate to make things easier for others.

Facilitate code changes

It's a great feeling to bring a project online for the first time to make it accessible to everyone. The desire to add features kept coming. I initially just changed the code, then replaced the files on the server with my newly created code. Everything was done manually.

Initially, I had no problems, everything was fine until an error report came from a user, I had trouble not being able to trace where the error came from. Restoring the last modified code was too late, I had already deleted the old code.

I learned a few techniques as my app grew. Each of the lines scared me at first, so I tried to avoid learning them for as long as possible until the right time came when I was overwhelmed by the code changes to be made.

Reminder: You can't be an expert in an instant, don't be afraid, and don't wait to understand each section below to start working, they can come another day.

Automated testing

You must run tests against your applications, not just once, you must retest the app whenever you add new features. Don't let the code you add, fix or reduce break the previous feature. For this reason, you need to create automated testing. Testing packages are available for all program languages.

Automated testing is a process to test all possible cases in your code. More people are creating apps to facilitate automated testing.

For example, when users open an application, what should they see or what should happen when a user registers, you write codes on all these cases and the desired results.

I was skeptical of doing this, I thought I was just doing the job twice. Wait until your project gets bigger and you get more unpredicted error reports.

By doing this, when you change your code, you'll be safe in the knowledge that with just one command, you can run all the tests automatically and get the reports that would have been done manually.

"Fixing the bug is usually pretty quick - finding it is a nightmare" - Martin Fowler.

Version control system

Before changing the code, a tool can help you, namely VCS or Version Control System. The most popular distributed version control system is Git.

VCS is just like playing a game, where there are checkpoints to store data. When a problem occurs, for example, your character dies, you don't need to start over from the beginning, you can play again starting from the checkpoint.

In the coding world, when you completed a feature, you can save it in VCS.

It's like having multiple versions of your code that you can always go back to, in case of problems occur with the manipulated code in the future.

Apart from being a checkpoint, VCS can also be used when you work in teams or are required to create features without interfering with the current application.

It allows you to create a payment feature and a profile change feature at the same time.

You can prevent crashes or may not be puzzled about what causes the error. VCS can reduce your burden.

VCS also often comes with an app. It allows you to visually compare where you made code changes, deletions or additions since the last time you saved the code. This brings a sense of peace of mind to play further with your code.

Activity log

Recording user activity is called logging. Logging their activity allows you to track when and where errors occur.

You can manually create the code or utilize a library/plugin depending on the programming language, I recommend the latter.

At present, there are many applications offering user activity logging, you just have to follow your own method.

Continuous deployment

Continuous Deployment allows you and the team to make changes when the application is online or used by real users. The faster the change process to the user, the better the system.

The bigger your team gets or the more features you want to develop simultaneously, the more forked your code created with VCS becomes. It's not as easy as when it's all one-way, you make a change and it goes straight to the user.

You now need to pay close attention to where your changes are made and whether they interfere with other features.

This part can include a powerful combination of VCS and automated testing.

In general, due to the ease of integrating new features or code changes, you (the team) will be more eager to continue to the next challenge. Imagine if you had a new desired feature to use, but because of the long integration time, you ended up having to wait. The longer you wait, the more code to review and integrate. Eventually, it's more difficult and takes longer time to bring new changes to users.

Therefore, it is necessary to make the change system as efficient as possible.

Learn to code together

After a few months of learning coding at Freecodecamp, I talked with my buddy Levi, who was studying at the same college but in different majors. We agreed to work together to improve our coding skills. Levi and I practically shared the same activities, notably college (though I rarely attend) and working, and we are fortunate to have a side career as programmers.

Saturday was the ideal time for us to sit down and learn to program. We chose one of Berlin's libraries as a spot to 'hack' together; if we just had a few hours, we would meet at my apartment, do some work, have a talk, and then go out for a bite to eat.

When we first started working, we could easily spend hours. It's natural to argue and admire one another. Having a code partner that you would consider a competitor is quite beneficial.

This appeared to be one of my most rapid growth stages.

We could argue why the code was flawed and how to make it better. We got out of our restricted perspective and expertise through coding together, and we were ready to hear and argue for other people's perspectives.

A few years later, while researching various ways of a programmer working in a corporation, I discovered two things that were similar to what we were doing without having any prior knowledge of the theory, namely Pair Programming and Code Review.

Pair Programming and Code Review

Pair Programming and Core Review are different, but they are of the same essence. The written code involves more than one person. The first one, pair programming, means that programmers code together, using the same machine and screen (if they are in the same location).

This method allows us to be more careful because we feel that someone is watching us. An error may occur, but with 4 or more people, simple mistakes can be weeded out early on and the best solution can be found as early as possible because the coding is accompanied by discussion.

Typically, there is also a navigator of the two people. The navigator may explain the program to be created or create automated testing to ensure all cases will be met.

Meanwhile, Code Review means you write the code first before being seen and reviewed by another person to get better results.

At this level, the person reviewing is a senior (who has more experience than you) because, with his experience, he already knows what can be fixed.

You don't have to wait to work to do the two tasks, from now on, you can look for partners at the same level to perform Pair Programming or find people better at coding, ask them to give feedback on the code (code review) that you have written.

If you don't have any idea where to find them, look around you, ask your friends, join either online or offline community.

First principle

a person enjoying instant coffee may be limited to the taste of the instant coffee. He can only taste two variations of coffee, either cold or hot coffee. Unlike a person seeking to find out the actual coffee, he might realize that coffee comes from a variety of coffee beans.

Each geographic origin, type, and processing method can offer different coffee flavors. Not to mention when mixed with other ingredients such as milk, palm sugar and many more.

The difference between the two people is that one just knows and another uses the first principle.

People who know about computers through advertisements may save money to buy computers.

However, a person who finds out what a computer really is, what does a computer consist of?

He starts to break down the components that make up a computer so that he can make his own computer at a lower price.

The second person is the one using first-principles thinking.

This is what **Elon Musk** did, Elon was trying to understand why rockets were so expensive, he studied and asked experts, what are the components to make up the rocket and made an estimation of how much it would cost so that he could make it. In fact, the price could be much lower. Rockets that were just a child's fantasy are now one of Elon's ventures through SpaceX.

One of the key points if you want to learn **first principles thinking** is that you reject what most people say or just because 'it's always been that way'. You should be interested in breaking down a problem into smaller parts to be explored gradually.

A physics professor was famous for his unique character and ability to explain a theory, his name was Richard Feynman. The professor was highly interested in problems that he couldn't explain. He refused just to accept a theory from a book or experts, he wanted to fully understand the theory.

For this reason, he would break down a theory into smaller ones that he could understand one by one, before building them back up to the initial problem. This allowed Feynman to explain difficult concepts in simple terms.

"I don't know what's the matter with people: they don't learn by understanding, they learn by some other way — by rote or something. Their knowledge is so fragile!" - **Richard Feynman**

How do you learn?

I began to realize that all this time I was just like a parrot, shouting what I heard. Not all information is worthy of being knowledge, especially now that many people claim to be experts.

You need to rely on yourself, and start practicing to learn and use first principles thinking. Currently, the abundance of information media can cause cognitive biases.

You can hone this skill by relying on your current knowledge, whether you slavishly accept the knowledge or you've thought it through.

Take a piece of paper and write down the material you want to explore. Start pouring your knowledge on the material on the piece of paper.

You can break the material down into smaller pieces to help you get to a core issue.

When you ate fruits, you can explore where fruits come from, do they come from trees? why can trees grow? the soil? the sun? the water? by continuing to explore further, you do not only find out that the fruit is tasty, but you also find out how to grow trees to produce tasty fruits.

Needless to say, I'm not talking about real fruit, but the science you're interested in.

Learn from different fields

Generally, through proper observations and understanding a concept in a structured manner, you can acquire and implement knowledge from different fields.

Understanding how motors work and how to make a motorcycle move in can help you create other vehicles that are much different from motorcycles.

When you feel stuck on a problem, try to find inspiration by making an analogy, the analogy may help you define your problem and find a solution. Also, you must learn from people who have solved similar problems, albeit from different fields.

Be like a child

Look at the kids near you, they constantly ask questions, unless their parents don't answer their questions.

"Dad, what's that?"

"A tree," said his father.

"Why did the tree get so big?"

"Because it gets watered," answered his father again

"Why does it need watering?" asked the little boy.

"That's how it works, son," his father ended the conversation.

If parents end the conversation by saying 'that's the way it is' or 'it's just the way it's always been' to their children, they will shut the door of knowledge by not being interested in asking further questions.

We accept what has happened. In fact, not everything is good for you.

Imagine that you are a child playing with lego blocks, and you see the tube to stick Legos together. Lego has a variety of shapes and colors. Here, you can build something completely unique and different according to your imagination, because you know the 'basis' aka 'first principle' of a lego that can be assembled with each other.

Make your knowledge like the lego bricks, small, many and flexible. They can be put together into your unique strengths when others only know to build structures from Lego bricks according to lego instruction booklets.

Being a Human

Communication

One day, I was discussing with a friend from the same city, Denver. His business run well, but it used manual processes. He hadn't utilized technology for the business. I was interested in contributing with my skills because I found out that the business had helped people's economies and had the potential to grow in the future.

As a programmer, I have many ideas to create an application when I encounter such a problem. In fact, long before that, I need to identify the required needs.

Therefore, I asked permission to visit his office and do nothing other than talk to the respective team and gather information.

I found out how they worked from the moment the service opened, I took notes on what they were working on, asking as much detail as possible if there is anything unclear.

I had to restrain my ego, not to ask "what if we make X app?". Indeed, it's not easy, I tend to rush to conclusions. I forgot that we are given two eyes to see with, two ears to listen with, but only one mouth to speak with.

The second and subsequent days were no different, I slowly began to see the pattern of activity, and from there came the idea of how to facilitate their system with the help of technology.

I repeatedly asked them to take their time, just to talk and ask questions. It's hard to communicate while they were working, I could have missed important information.

Stop making assumptions

It is human nature to want to be heard when speaking and not the other way around.
It takes awareness and practice to listen to the other person.

However, we don't only listen, but also understand their problem because we offer service to help a company or a person.

Ask the details until you are satisfied and eliminate the culture of people pleasers, you should feel bad if you don't do the task optimally. To optimize the task, you need to understand the job well.

Likewise, when assigning a task to a junior or partner, you must describe the task as clearly as possible and eliminate the ambiguity that may lead to vague assumptions. Assumptions are a sign that you don't try to clarify the matter whereas it's your obligation.

Having different opinions

When you knew the way in a city, and a friend of yours was driving, he said "I'm going to turn right ahead", while you know exactly the road was being repaired, indicating a total traffic jam. As you feel bad, you say yes, and you end up stuck in traffic and late for your next activity.

Having different opinions is fine.

When you're working in a team, it would be weird and suspicious when you all have the same idea.

Some people just agree with others to avoid conflict, but it means that you keep your problems to yourself.

Honestly speak your mind, if you think your friend was wrong, say it!. In fact, you're not always right, so don't hesitate to argue with someone. Don't close your ears as you have your own opinion, someone else could be right or you might find a brighter way from a combination of both opinions.

Being afraid or reluctant to argue means being lazy. You will feel the effects of laziness in the future. Your project might be difficult to control, add features, and develop, and eventually, you have to go back to the drawing board.

Think like a programmer

A programmer should avoid DRY (Don't Repeat Yourself), not only in the programs that they are created but also in everyday life. Tasks or jobs that you do many times should be able to automate, observe carefully!

In my personal case:

- make daily database backups

- post content on the website to social media

- check payments or user transfers

- create social media content and much more!

These things seem trivial because they only take up a little time, but your focus is shifted every day. After making a list of everything that I do over and over again, I started to find one way or another to complete the tasks automatically. You and I certainly have different activities and problem solutions.

For instance, if you're working with clients, do you already have a pattern of your clients? is there any application or website to serve clients? Is it possible if you create a program to serve as the basic framework for all your subsequent programs so that for future work, you don't have to go back to the drawing board?

Make it easy on yourself!

The programmer's job is to make life easier with technology. In addition to programs that you have created, there are tons of apps out there that have been created by other developers to make particular activities easier.

People are more likely to save money than time. You can get more money, but you cannot get more time. Don't be so stingy about money, if there is an application that can make your life easier, don't hesitate to pay for the app. Using the app can save your time and you can do something better suited to your job.

Likewise, there is nothing wrong to look for free educational platforms to increase your knowledge. However, it is not right to not willing to pay for books or video courses with the excuse of saving a little money because they are sources of knowledge to increase your job knowledge that may result in an increase in income.

Start thinking like a program that is ready to make other people's lives easier, but this time, start by making it easier for yourself. Start investing time and money to improve your life.

Here are some questions inspired by Tim Ferris' The 4-Hour Workweek that may help you:

- Is there an easier way?

- Is there an app I can pay for to make things easier?

- Can this task be done by someone else that I paid for?

- Is this activity important or should I leave it?

One computer for life

What if you can only buy one computer for the rest of your life?

I'm sure you will be extremely careful using it, will take serious care of the software and hardware, and make sure it is safe from others.

You may have more than one computer in your life, but what about your body? God gives you one chance at life with physical health.

However, many people are not aware of their physical health. They stay up late every day, do smoke, consume soft drinks, do not exercise, and so on. People are willing to do anything to keep working, to refuel the body, even though the fuel may destroy them.

You only have one body with all its sophistication, including growing nails and hair, fully functioning organs, changes in body shape as you grow. You get all the things that scientists fail to reproduce for free. Do you take good care of everything that God has given to you for free?

Pomodoro technique

Eating a healthy diet and regular exercise has been a slogan since we were little. We haven't fully practiced it, but you might have heard the slogan. I will be sharing a rarely discussed technique, the Pomodoro technique.

The Pomodoro technique involves working for 20 minutes and taking a 5-minute break. Repeat the step, 25 minutes of work and 5 minutes of rest, repeat.

During 25-minute work intervals, you have to focus on your work by not using social media or mobile phones. You have to focus on doing one thing at a time, then take 5-minute rest, even though you're in the middle of your work. During the 5-minute rest, you can exercise your eyes, stand straight back or take a walk.

You may use applications (there are plenty of Podomoro apps, both apps and mobile websites) or use a regular alarm. The methods allow you to prevent slouching, tired eyes, an overworked brain, and many more. It looks easy, but it will be useful if you do it.

Or, try eye fixation as below

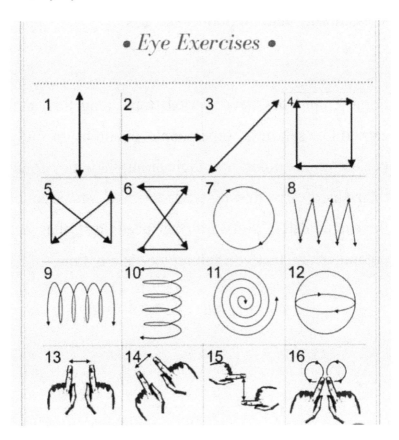

Don't forget to rest.

The Pomodoro technique is a simple tool to help you take a rest at work. When you have finished your work, give yourself a gift, buy your favorite food or drink, go for a walk to gain experience, or make time for your hobbies outside of your 9-5 job. The point is to make yourself happy, relieve your stress during and after doing the task.

Some employees have worked for a long time and earned low salaries. Some people sit and try to study but nothing is going into their brain, they may force their 'hardware' to work, do not take into account their overheated 'software' that needs rest, they are not a machine that you can replace at any time.

It is normal to feel tired.

Evolving technology has two different impacts on us. On one hand, it has a positive impact because constantly evolving software and hardware can make work easier. On the other hand, to keep up with the developments, you may often feel left behind which often ends up feeling stupid and blaming yourself.

When you feel that way, don't worry, you are not alone, many people are going through the same thing. This is called the "Fear of Missing Out" FOMO. When you read all the news and try to learn everything, just because you are worried that you can't keep up with a discussion between friends or look stupid.

In fact, no one can do everything. In fact, it's common for people to become tired.

This feeling makes you feel like you're working endlessly, you have to keep working and learning.

As a result, you spend less time with family, let alone for yourself.

To overcome the problem, focus on the work that you need to complete because it's your main objective. The rest will follow, it doesn't matter if you don't know the latest and emerging X technology, just let it be, you can read the news later. Focus on completing the task at hand.

By focusing on completing the current task, your mind will not be disturbed and you will feel relieved when it is finished. Conversely, if the mandatory task is not completed, your mind will be chaotic, you will get panicked and be unable to do anything. Therefore, stop doing multiple things at once, focus on one task at a time.

You only live for a very short time, if you spend time chasing people and trying to please everyone, you will be carried away until your time runs out. Be yourself! you know your need, you don't have to look great in everyone's eyes. Do a good job, get ready to create, do your hobby, take a break when needed, and enjoy the process! You will get tired when running, that's normal. Please take a rest and continue at your own pace.

Impostor Syndrome

Even though I have taught programming for years, the "I don't deserve to do this" feeling is still there. It stresses me out, I can't learn, make materials, or teach. Likewise, when I was invited to an event to share materials, either as a speaker or jury, the feeling of "I commit fraud to others" will emerge as if I'm just waiting for someone to take off the mask I'm wearing and everyone will eventually know that I can't do anything.

I started looking for the problem, back in 1978, Pauline Rose and Suzanne Ament had researched and written about this, which was called the "impostor syndrome". In their journal, it was stated that regardless of tangible evidence of career achievements or awards recognized by others, many women continue to feel "impostor syndrome", the feeling of committing fraud on others (not deserving of anything) and just lucky to get through all the previous challenges. This study focuses on women because women are more likely to experience impostor syndrome than men.

the word "**imposter**" it's a rude word and is painful to hear it. But to be honest, the real feeling of "I don't deserve to share an experience or I don't deserve to be in my current job" often emerges. I feel "just lucky" to get here, not because I tried and deserved it.

Impostor Syndrome is a feeling that emerges as if you deceive others with what you are doing, regardless of your real achievements. This makes you feel inferior and cause stress to work that you actually love.

Things that may cause Imposter Syndrome

Anne Lamott once wrote, *"don't compare yourself to how you look on the outside"*. Unfortunately, this is exactly what you do. You knew yourself from childhood, knew the shortcomings and mistakes that were often made.

The problem arises when you compare with what other people see. What you see is not the "real side" of other people. You only see their success or what they choose to share in the virtual world. It's like comparing apples and fried chicken. THEY ARE DIFFERENT.

An unsupportive environment may also cause Imposter Syndrome.

Since childhood, your achievements are often considered "insignificant" by others. Score 90 is not sufficient, you have to get a score of 100. You live with criticism that keeps ringing in your ears if you can't do anything.

Types of Impostor Syndrome

If you don't feel the same way as I feel, there are several symptoms of Impostor Syndrome:

- Feeling stupid and hard to learn. Feeling that other people are so much better.
- Looking for excuses that other people are talented, but he is not. For example, when you see Lionel Messi playing football, you may say that he is talented. In fact, Messi has been doing a lot more training than you.
- You have to create a masterpiece. This statement is nonsense, you will never be perfect. You will end up punishing yourself. You will end up punishing yourself and be sad when you get a score of 99 out of 100, 1 more point to achieve a score of 100. You might forget to celebrate and enjoy the results of your efforts.
- Feeling you are not unique. All matters have been voiced by someone else, you are no longer needed.

The feelings are signs of impostor syndrome.

Is it dangerous to have imposter syndrome?

Yes. It's very dangerous. The feeling will prevent you from making any important decision. For example, I didn't want to write this in the first place because I didn't feel like an expert.

Expressing your opinion may help other depressed people. It may not help everyone, but some people need your opinion.

You are hiding in your comfort zone, don't want to do anything, don't have to try anything new, just follow other people's orders and give up on everything.

You dare not speak, dare not to lead. Eventually, you give up on the situation, have no confidence to optimize your potential or blame others for your own actions.

Other disturbances will follow you every day such as excessive worry, fear, shame, lack of confidence to depression to live a life.

As a matter of fact, it is not appropriate to say that having impostor syndrome is dangerous. It is common to experience the symptoms, it is just a matter of how you react to them. You must not stop your work after experiencing the symptoms of impostor syndrome.

One tip from **Mike Cannon-Brookes**, a billionaire from Australia, when you are aware that you are experiencing the disease, be grateful, do your best, learn and try to optimize your potentials.

Mike stated that he experienced the syndrome after marriage, he felt that he didn't deserve his wife. It doesn't mean that he has to divorce her, but he should be grateful and try to be a proper husband for his   wife.

How to deal with impostor syndrome?

The good news is that you and I are not the only ones experiencing the syndrome. Some expert authors also experienced the impostor syndrome, including Anne Lamott, Maya Angelou, Steven Pressfield, Elizabeth Gilbert, and many other authors. Despite their numerous bestselling books, they feel "inappropriate" and "commit of fraud to others". This doesn't only occur in the art world, but also in the other fields.

There are a few things we can do to solve the problem (not completely eliminate it):

- Realize that the feeling is real and is felt by many people. WE ARE NOT ALONE.
- Talking about your feeling with friends or family, not hiding your feeling that may lead to stress.

- Try to look perfect in the eyes of others will be a burden. Get in the habit of asking for help and don't be shy to learn from others.
- Change your mindset that we are lifelong learners. We are still in the development phase and will never finish learning. There will be drawbacks and that's not a problem.
- Appreciate your own efforts. Don't just look at the end result. At the end of the day, you can't control the results. appreciate the things that you can control, your efforts.
- Realize that we can't be perfect in everything. Being a programmer does not mean that I am an expert in speaking. And don't make excuses: because I'm bad at A, that means I can't do B
- Remember that we were not created by God in vain. The fact that we are alive today means that there is still an opportunity to do the work that we should be doing.

In whatever position we are in, just starting to struggle or already in a comfortable career position, the impostor syndrome occurs. Don't underestimate yourself, problems come with various conveniences.

Now, it is your turn.

Our job is not only coding in front of the screen. The skills and knowledge will be wasteful if you only use them yourself. Make something out of this power of yours. You can always share knowledge with others, write a blog, share knowledge in seminars, make videos or podcasts, all of which are wide open for you.

Feelings of inappropriateness will definitely come, but you are the one who decides whether to keep up the effort or give up due to the feeling. There are already enough problems in the world.

The world already has enough problems. The world lacks people who want to solve problems. You can see yourself as a hero, who doesn't care whether your name will be remembered or not, but who cares about the problem at hand and wants to solve it.

You can see yourself as an artist, someone whose work is enjoyed by many people. Present your best work. The computer is your stage and you're the actor. Now, you should go to the stage to perform. Everyone's been waiting.

It doesn't matter if you decide not to be a programmer now or forever. To be honest, I'm also not sure that I'll be a programmer forever, but I will never regret being a programmer. I have superpowers to solve the few problems in the world.

I consider that what I have shared so far as a gift. I have received many gifts from other people, in the form of knowledge or opportunities. I want to share the gifts with more people.

What about you?

What gifts have you prepared for other people?

I'm waiting for your gift.

Epilogue: You Can Do This

If there's one message I want to leave you with here, it is this: **you can do this.**

You can learn these concepts.

You can learn these tools.

You can become a developer.

Then, the moment someone hands you money for you to help them code something, you will graduate to being a professional developer.

Learning to code and getting a first developer job is a daunting process. But do not be daunted.

If you stick with it, you will eventually succeed. It is just a matter of practice.

Build your projects. Show them to your friends. Build projects for your friends.

Build your network. Help the people you meet along the way. What goes around comes around. You'll get what's coming to you.

It is not too late. Life is long.

You will look back on this moment years from now and be glad you made a move.

Plan for it to take a long time. Plan for uncertainty.

But above all, keep coming back to the keyboard. Keep making it out to events. Keep sharing your wins with friends.

As **Lao Tzu**, the Old Master, once said:

"A journey of a thousand miles begins with a single step."

By finishing this book, you've already taken a step. Heck, you may have already taken many steps toward your goals.

Momentum is everything. So keep up that forward momentum you've already built up over these past few hours with this book.

Start coding your next project today.

And always remember:

You can do this.

1. *Dont quit 5 minutes before the miracle happens*
2. *Failure if not an option*
3. *Remember when you see at the top of a mountain, he didn't fall there*
4. *The best place to find a helping hand is at the end of your own arm*
5. *There are 3 kind of people ; (1) Those who want it (2) Those who say it never shall work (3) those who do it*
6. *Failure is not falling down*
7. *Knowing is not enough; we must apply, Willing is not enough; we must do*

The Author

After 9 years of work as a forklift operator, locksmith-fitter, grinder, and welder, among others, decided to change his career and started working as a Front-end Developer.

Today, i have almost 2 years of work experience, has doubled his previous earnings, and carries out projects for American companies from Silicon Valley. I've done a lot of things - for a total of about nine years. My first serious job was production work in my small hometown. I was 20 years old at the time. It was just ordinary work at a conveyor belt, but it was freezing because the work took place in a cold store.

After a few months there, I snatched a job as a forklift operator because I had already gotten my qualifications when I was considering moving to Postdam to study, thinking it would help me get a job in order to stay there.

After arriving in Postdam germany, thanks to my cousin's help, I found employment in a security company as an ordinary security guard in one of the supermarkets in a shopping mall. This was a good job to get me on my feet so I could start looking for something more serious and better paid because EUR 1.5 per hour wasn't much.

After two months, I managed to find a job as a locksmith-fitter, where I had the opportunity to learn to weld.

I did so, and after a year and a half on the job, I moved into a welder-grinder position. After a little more than four years, I changed my company to a better one and continued to practice this profession. I didn't stay there for too long (1.5 years), and while working there, I started learning JavaScript programming. So, that would be (hopefully) my last manual job before starting work as a Frontend Developer.

James Rivaldo Martin

Bibliography

Martin, Robert C. Clean Code. Pearson. 2008

Thomas, Dave,. Hunt, Andy. The Pragmatic
Programmer. Addison-Wesley. 1999

Fowler, Martin,. Beck, Kent. Refactoring. Addison-
Wesley. 1999

Katia. (July, 2020) From Baker to Software
Engineer

www.ingramcontent.com/pod-product-compliance
Lightning Source LLC
LaVergne TN
LVHW052059060326
832903LV00060B/2286